The Letters of the Hangul Alphabet

The Korean script is called Hangul. It was invented by King Sejong the Great in 1444. He wanted to come up with an easy writing system that everyone could use to read and write the Korean language. Before this time, only scholars and the ruling class could read and write. King Sejong wanted all his citizens to be literate and to have a better life. Hangul did just that, uniting the social classes of Korea.

The consonants (**C**) and vowels (**V**) in the charts below are combined to make syllables, just as in English. Korean syllables are formed using the following combinations: **C + V** or **C + V + C**

Note: There are no letters for the sounds f, v and z in Hangul.

Consonants (TRACK 1)

Basic	ㄱ	ㄴ	ㄷ	ㄹ	ㅁ	ㅂ	ㅅ	ㅇ	ㅈ
	g or k	n	d or t	r or l	m	b or p	s or sh	ng	j or ch
Double	ㄲ		ㄸ			ㅃ	ㅆ		ㅉ
	kk		tt			pp	ss		jj
Heavy	ㅋ		ㅌ			ㅍ		ㅎ	ㅊ
	k		t			p		h	ch

Vowels (TRACK 2)

Single	ㅏ		ㅓ		ㅣ	ㅗ	ㅜ	ㅡ	
	a		eo		i	o	u	eu	
Double	ㅑ	ㅐ	ㅒ	ㅕ	ㅔ	ㅖ		ㅛ	ㅠ
	ya	ae	yae	yeo	e	ye		yo	yu
	ㅘ	ㅙ	ㅚ	ㅝ	ㅞ	ㅟ	ㅢ		
	wa	wae	oe	weo	we	wi	ui		

Chart Showing Consonant + Vowel Combinations

This chart shows the most commonly used consonants and vowels of the Hangul alphabet, and how they are combined to make syllables. The consonants are on the left axis of the chart and the vowels are along the top. The combinations are shown in the table.

Vowels / Consonants	ㅏ a	ㅑ ya	ㅓ eo	ㅕ yeo	ㅗ o	ㅛ yo	ㅜ u	ㅠ yu	ㅡ eu	ㅣ i
ㄱ g	가 ga	갸 gya	거 geo	겨 gyeo	고 go	교 gyo	구 gu	규 gyu	그 geu	기 gi
ㄴ n	나 na	냐 nya	너 neo	녀 nyeo	노 no	뇨 nyo	누 nu	뉴 nyu	느 neu	니 ni
ㄷ d	다 da	댜 dya	더 deo	뎌 dyeo	도 do	됴 dyo	두 du	듀 dyu	드 deu	디 di
ㄹ l (r)	라 la	랴 lya	러 leo	려 lyeo	로 lo	료 lyo	루 lu	류 lyu	르 leu	리 li
ㅁ m	마 ma	먀 mya	머 meo	며 myeo	모 mo	묘 myo	무 mu	뮤 myu	므 meu	미 mi
ㅂ b	바 ba	뱌 bya	버 beo	벼 byeo	보 bo	뵤 byo	부 bu	뷰 byu	브 beu	비 bi
ㅅ s	사 sa	샤 sya	서 seo	셔 syeo	소 so	쇼 syo	수 su	슈 syu	스 seu	시 si
ㅇ silent	아 a	야 ya	어 eo	여 yeo	오 o	요 yo	우 u	유 yu	으 eu	이 i
ㅈ j	자 ja	쟈 jya	저 jeo	져 jyeo	조 jo	죠 jyo	주 ju	쥬 jyu	즈 jeu	지 ji
ㅊ ch	차 cha	챠 chya	처 cheo	쳐 chyeo	초 cho	쵸 chyo	추 chu	츄 chyu	츠 cheu	치 chi
ㅋ k	카 ka	캬 kya	커 keo	켜 kyeo	코 ko	쿄 kyo	쿠 ku	큐 kyu	크 keu	키 ki
ㅌ t	타 ta	탸 tya	터 teo	텨 tyeo	토 to	툐 tyo	투 tu	튜 tyu	트 teu	티 ti
ㅍ p	파 pa	퍄 pya	퍼 peo	펴 pyeo	포 po	표 pyo	푸 pu	퓨 pyu	프 peu	피 pi
ㅎ h	하 ha	햐 hya	허 heo	혀 hyeo	호 ho	효 hyo	후 hu	휴 hyu	흐 heu	히 hi
ㄲ kk	까 kka	꺄 kkya	꺼 kkeo	껴 kkyeo	꼬 kko	꾜 kkyo	꾸 kku	뀨 kkyu	끄 kkeu	끼 kki
ㄸ tt	따 tta	땨 ttya	떠 tteo	뗘 ttyeo	또 tto	뚀 ttyo	뚜 ttu	뜌 ttyu	뜨 tteu	띠 tti
ㅃ pp	빠 ppa	뺘 ppya	뻐 ppeo	뼈 ppyeo	뽀 ppo	뾰 ppyo	뿌 ppu	쀼 ppyu	쁘 ppeu	삐 ppi
ㅉ jj	짜 jja	쨔 jjya	쩌 jjeo	쪄 jjyeo	쪼 jjo	쬬 jjyo	쭈 jju	쮸 jjyu	쯔 jjeu	찌 jji
ㅆ ss	싸 ssa	쌰 ssya	써 sseo	쎠 ssyeo	쏘 sso	쑈 ssyo	쑤 ssu	쓔 ssyu	쓰 sseu	씨 ssi

Practice Writing Hangul Letters

Forming the letters of Korean alphabet is easy! There are just two basic rules: horizontal strokes are written from left to right and vertical strokes are written from top to bottom, just as in English.

Let's write the consonants:

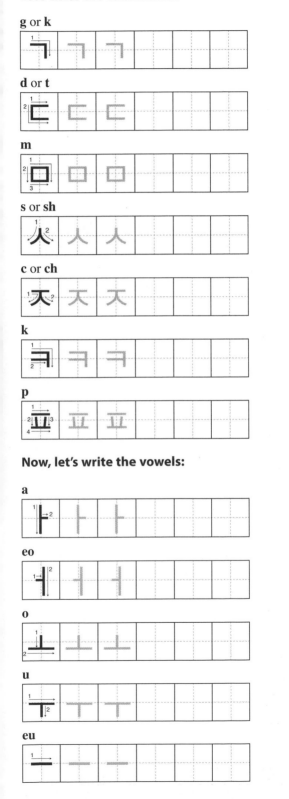
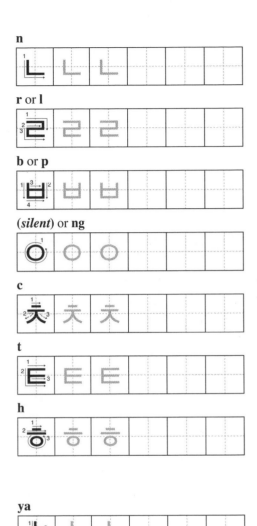

g or **k**

n

d or **t**

r or **l**

m

b or **p**

s or **sh**

(silent) or **ng**

c or **ch**

c

k

t

p

h

Now, let's write the vowels:

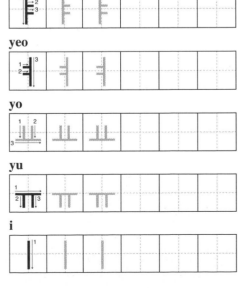

a

ya

eo

yeo

o

yo

u

yu

eu

i

3

Practice Writing Korean Syllables

Consonant + Vertical Vowel

The vertical vowels ㅏ, ㅓ and ㅣ are written to the right of the consonant, as in the following examples.

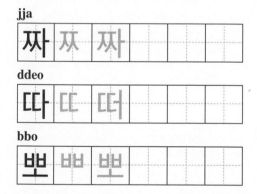

Consonant + Horizontal Vowel

Horizontal vowels ㅗ, ㅜ and ㅡ are written under the consonant, as in the following examples.

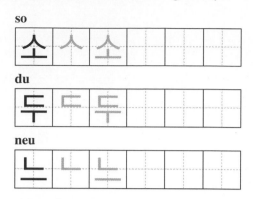

Double Consonant + Single Vowel

Write the double consonant first. If the vowel is vertical, write it on the right. If the vowel is horizontal, write it underneath.

Double Consonant + Double Vowel

Write the double consonant first. If the vowel is vertical, write it on the right. If the vowel is horizontal, write it underneath.

Heavy Consonant + Single or Double Vowel

The heavy consonants (k, t, p and h) are pronounced with a breath of air. Write the consonant first. If the vowel is vertical, write it to the right of the consonant. If the vowel is horizontal, write it underneath.

hi

kyeo

tyeo

Consonant + Vowel + Consonant (CVC)

In a CVC syllable, the final consonant is written under the vowel. (Sometimes this pattern has two final consonants as in the last two examples below.)

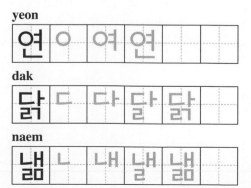

4

Everyday Words and Phrases

안녕하세요 **annyeong haseyo**   Hello

안녕하세요

환영합니다 **hwanyeonghapnida**   Welcome

환영합니다

들어오세요 **deureooseyo**   Please come in

들어오세요

잘 지냈어요? **jal jinaesseoyo?**   How have you been?

잘 지냈어요

잘 지냈어요 **jal jinaesseoyo**   I've been well

잘 지냈어요

괜찮습니다 **gwaenchanseupnida**   It's ok

괜찮습니다

감사합니다 **gamsahapnida**   Thank you

감사합니다

실례합니다 **sillyehapnida**   Excuse me

실례합니다

죄송합니다 **joesonghapnida**   I am sorry

죄송합니다

안녕히 가세요 **annyeonghi gaseyo**   Goodbye (to person leaving)

안녕히 가세요

안녕히 계세요 **annyeonghi gyeseyo**   Goodbye (to person staying)

안녕히 계세요

5

Hanging Out with K-Pop Fans

친구 **chingu** friend

친구								

한류 **hallyu** Korean Wave

한류								

입덕 **ipdeok** entering a fandom

입덕								

굿즈 **gutjeu** goods

굿즈								

대박! **daebak** Amazing! (lit. jackpot)

대박								

찐팬 **jjinpaen** big fan

찐팬								

팬질 **paenjil** doing fan activities

팬질								

팬싸 **paenssa** fan signing event

팬싸								

생일 **saengnil** birthday

생일								

팬클럽 **paenkeulleop** fan club

팬클럽						

팬미팅   **paenmiting**   fan meeting

팬 미 팅

팬카페   **paenkape**   online fan community (lit. fan café)

팬 카 페

진짜요?   **jinjjayo**   Is it true?

진 짜 요

화이팅!   **hwaiting**   Good luck! (lit. fighting)

화 이 팅

팬이에요   **paenieyo**   (I am) a fan (of …)

팬 이 에 요

축하해요   **chukahaeyo**   Congratulations

축 하 해 요

안녕하세요?   **annyeonghaseyo**   Hello

안 녕 하 세 요

또 만나요   **tto mannayo**   See you again

또 만 나 요

유튜브를 봐요   **yutyubeureul bwayo**   (I) watch YouTube videos

유 튜 브 를 봐 요

노래를 들어요   **noraereul deureoyo**   (I) listen to song(s)

노 래 를 들 어 요

Words and Phrases You Hear in K-Dramas

소주 **soju** soju

| 소 | 주 | | | | | | | | | | | | | | | | | | | |

치킨 **chikin** fried chicken

| 치 | 킨 | | | | | | | | | | | | | | | | | | | |

치맥 **chimaek** a pairing of fried chicken and beer

| 치 | 맥 | | | | | | | | | | | | | | | | | | | |

건배! **geonbae** Cheers!

| 건 | 배 | | | | | | | | | | | | | | | | | | | |

엄청 **eomcheong** very

| 엄 | 청 | | | | | | | | | | | | | | | | |

케이드라마 **keideurama** K-Drama

| 케 | 이 | 드 | 라 | 마 | | | | | | | | | | | | |

짜증나 **jjajeungna** It's annoying (informal)

| 짜 | 증 | 나 | | | | | | | | | | | | | | | |

어떡해! **eotteokae** Oh, no!

| 어 | 떡 | 해 | | | | | | | | | | | | | | | |

울지 마 **ulji ma** Don't cry (informal)

| 울 | 지 | 마 | | | | | | | | | | | | | | | |

맛있어요 **masisseoyo** It's tasty

| 맛 | 있 | 어 | 요 | | | | | | | | | | | | | | |

8

사랑해요 saranghaeyo I love (you)

사랑해요

왜 그래요? wae geuraeyo What's happening?

왜 그래요

보고 싶어요 bogo sipeoyo I miss (you)

보고 싶어요

남친 있어요 namchin isseoyo (I) have a boyfriend

남친 있어요

여친 있어요 yeochin isseoyo (I) have a girlfriend

여친 있어요

노래방 가자 noraebang gaja Let's go to noraebang (informal)

노래방 가자

밥 먹었어요? bap meogeosseoyo Have you eaten?

밥 먹었어요

한 잔 할래요? han jan hallaeyo Would you like a drink?

한 잔 할래요

너한테 빠졌어 neohante ppajyeosseo I've fallen into you (informal)

너한테 빠졌어

나랑 결혼해요 narang gyeolhonhaeyo Please marry me

나랑 결혼해요

Words and Phrases from Your Favorite K-Pop Songs

꿈 **kkum** dream

늘 **neul** always

음악 **eumak** music

느낌 **neukkim** feeling

비밀 **bimil** secret

우리 **uri** we

얘기 **yaegi** story, talk

추억 **chueok** memory

운명 **unmyeong** destiny

케이팝 **keipap** K-Pop

너와 같이 **neowa gachi**   with you

너와 같이

괜찮아요 **gwaenchanayo**   (I am) alright

괜찮아요

미안해요 **mianhaeyo**   I am sorry

미안해요

약속해요 **yaksokaeyo**   I promise

약속해요

좋아해요 **joahaeyo**   I like (you)

좋아해요

너무 소중해요 **neomu sojunghae**   (You're) so precious (to me)

너무 소중해요

걱정하지 마 **geokjeonghaji ma**   Don't worry (informal)

걱정하지 마

멈추지 않아 **meomchuji ana**   We won't stop (informal)

멈추지 않아

내 손을 잡아 **nae soneul jaba**   Hold my hand (informal)

내 손을 잡아

영원히 함께니까 **yeongwonhi hamkkenikka**   (We will) be together forever (informal)

영원히 함께니까

🎧 TRACK 8 Talking about Idols

오빠 **oppa** older brother (of a female)

오빠								

누나 **nuna** older sister (of a male)

누나								

최애 **choeae** one's favorite

최애								

심쿵 **simkung** having a crush (lit. heart + booming)

심쿵								

애교 **aegyo** acting cute

애교								

배우 **baeu** actor

배우								

가수 **gasu** singer

가수								

컴백 **keombaek** coming back with new music

컴백								

아이돌 **aidol** idol

아이돌			

꽃미남 **kkonminam** beautiful boy (lit. flower boy)

꽃미남			

꽃미녀　**kkonminyeo**　pretty girl (lit. flower girl)

꽃미녀

예뻐요　**yeppeoyo**　(someone) is pretty

예뻐요

잘생겼어요　**jalsaenggyeosseoyo**　(someone) is handsome

잘생겼어요

인스타그램　**inseutageuraem**　Instagram

인스타그램

팔로우해요　**pallouhaeyo**　(I) follow

팔로우해요

티켓팅 해요　**tiketting haeyo**　(I) buy tickets

티켓팅해요

영통팬싸 해요　**yeongtongpaenssa haeyo**　(I) do a video call with idols

영통팬싸해요

춤을 잘 춰요　**chumeul jal chwoyo**　(someone) dances well

춤을잘춰요

노래를 잘해요　**noraereul jalhaeyo**　(someone) sings well

노래를잘해요

연기를 잘해요　**yeongireul jalhaeyo**　(someone) acts well

연기를잘해요

Useful Verbs

가요 **gayo** (I) go

가	요												

와요 **wayo** (I) come

와	요												

쥐요 **jwoyo** (I) give

쥐	요												

들려요 **deullyeoyo** (I) hear

들	려	요									

알아요 **arayo** (I) know

알	아	요									

웃어요 **useoyo** (I) smile

웃	어	요									

마셔요 **masyeoyo** (I) drink

마	셔	요									

말해요 **malhaeyo** (I) say

말	해	요									

몰라요 **mollayo** (I) do not know

몰	라	요									

빛나요 **binnayo** (it) shines

빛	나	요									

원해요 **wonhaeyo** (I) want

원 해 요

즐겨요 **jeulgyeoyo** (I) enjoy

즐 겨 요

찾아요 **chajayo** (I) find

찾 아 요

고마워요 **gomawoyo** (I) thank

고 마 워 요

기억해요 **gieokaeyo** (I) remember

기 억 해 요

기다려요 **gidaryeoyo** (I) wait

기 다 려 요

노래해요 **noraehaeyo** (I) sing

노 래 해 요

생각해요 **saenggakaeyo** (I) think

생 각 해 요

이해해요 **ihaehaeyo** (I) understand

이 해 해 요

안아줘요 **anajwoyo** (I) hug

안 아 줘 요

TRACK 10 🎧 Useful Adjectives

기뻐요 **gippeoyo** (I am) glad

기	뻐	요														

달라요 **dallayo** (it is) different

달	라	요														

많아요 **manayo** There are a lot

많	아	요														

아파요 **apayo** (I am) ill

아	파	요														

슬퍼요 **seulpeoyo** (I am) sad

슬	퍼	요														

신나요 **sinnayo** (I am) excited

신	나	요														

매워요 **maewoyo** (it is) spicy

매	워	요														

좋아요 **joayo** (it is) good

좋	아	요														

나빠요 **nappayo** (it is) bad

나	빠	요														

귀여워요 **gwiyeowoyo** (it is) cute

귀	여	워	요												

다정해요   **dajeonghaeyo**   (someone) is kind

다	정	해	요									

달콤해요   **dalkomhaeyo**   (it is) sweet

달	콤	해	요									

외로워요   **oerowoyo**   (I am) lonely

외	로	워	요									

지루해요   **jiruhaeyo**   (it is) boring

지	루	해	요									

따뜻해요   **ttatteutaeyo**   (it is) warm

따	뜻	해	요									

특별해요   **teukbyeolhaey**   (it is) special

특	별	해	요									

행복해요   **haengbokaeyo**   (I am) happy

행	복	해	요									

아름다워요   **areumdawoyo**   (it is) beautiful

아	름	다	워	요					

재미있어요   **jaemiisseoyo**   (it is) interesting

재	미	있	어	요					

사랑스러워요   **sarangseureowoyo**   (it is) lovely

사	랑	스	러	워	요			

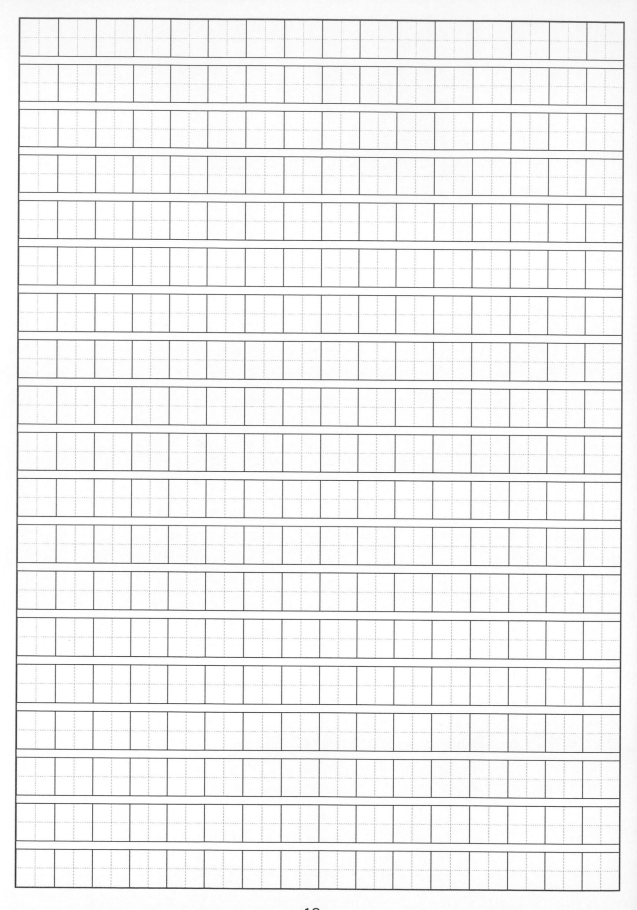

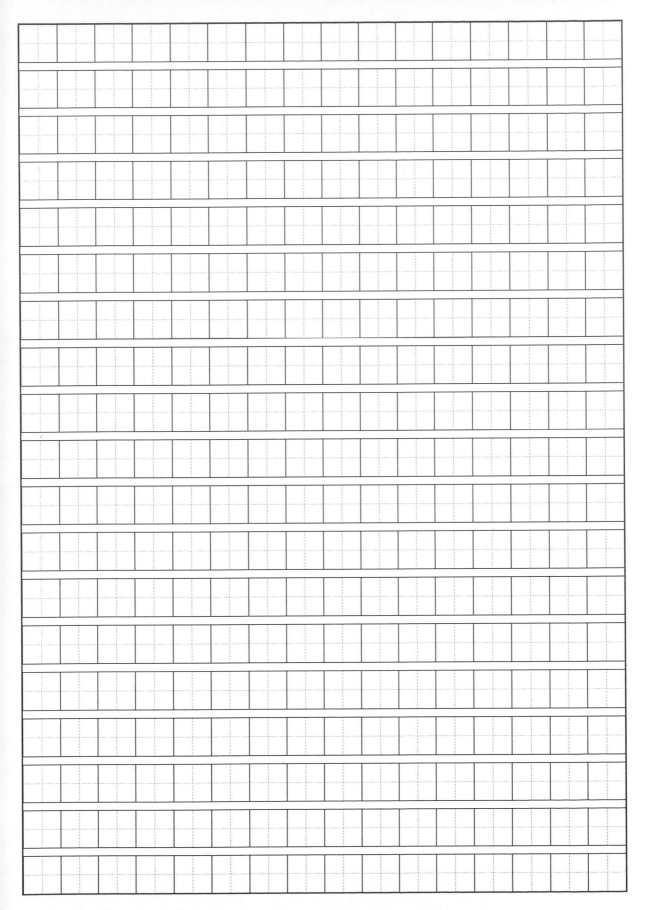

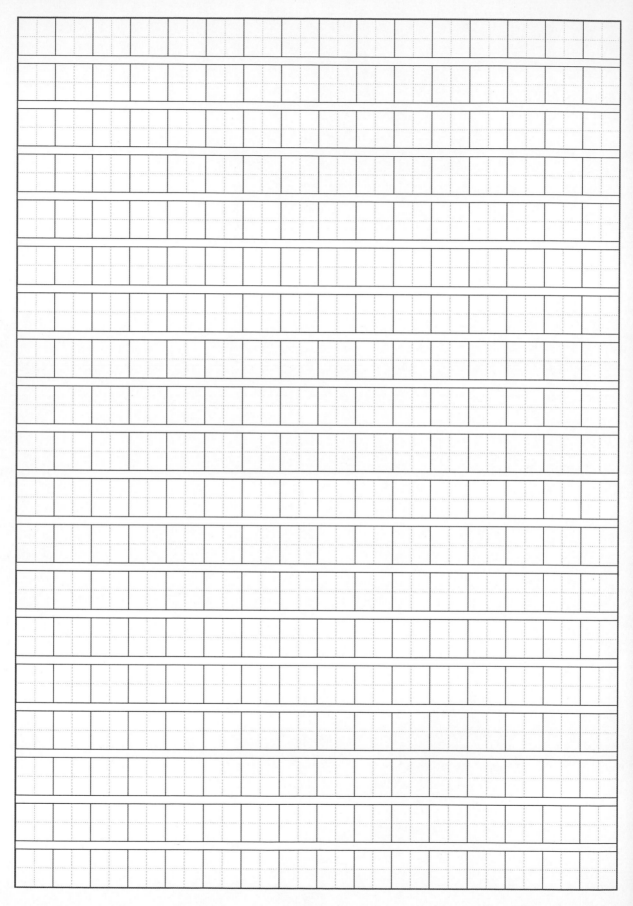

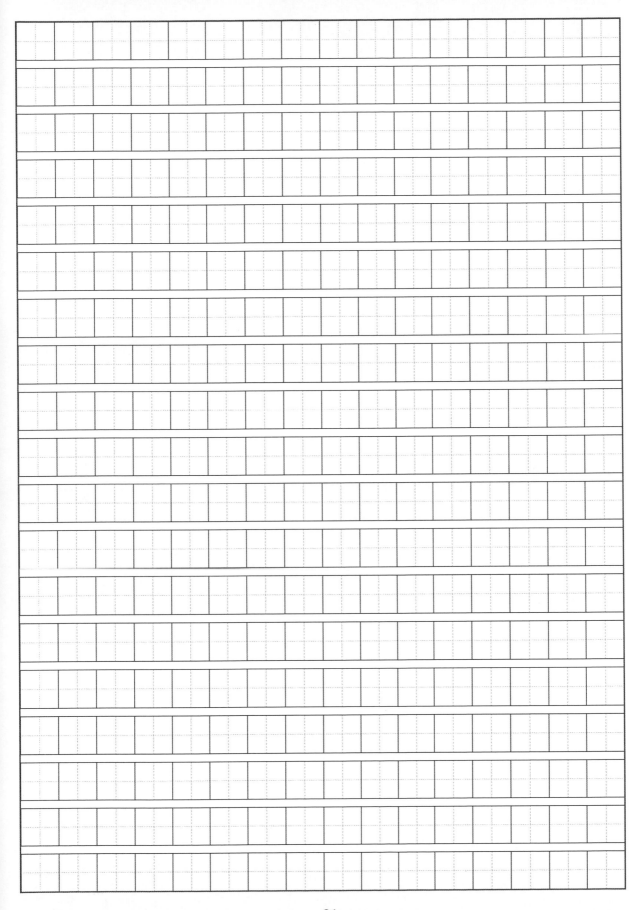

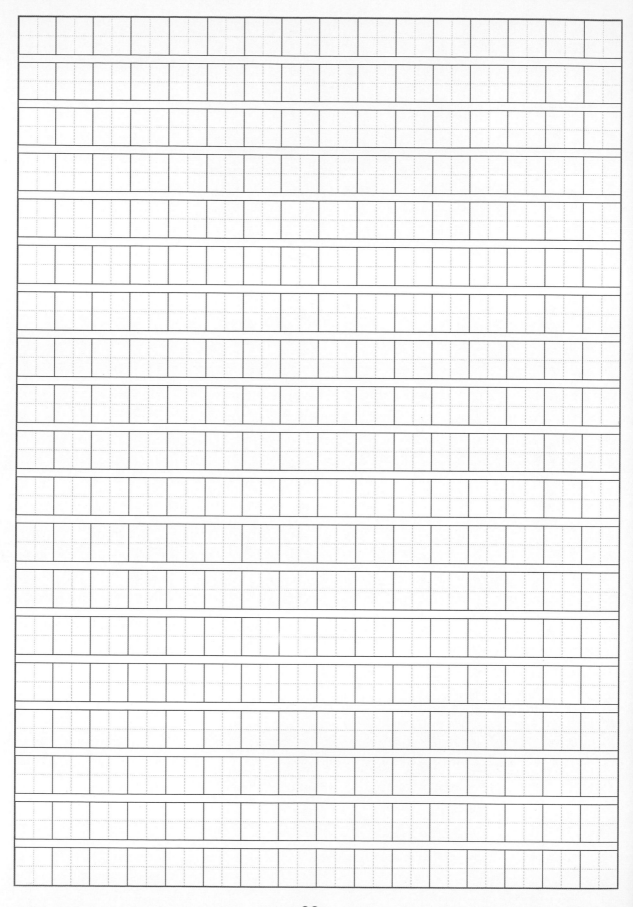

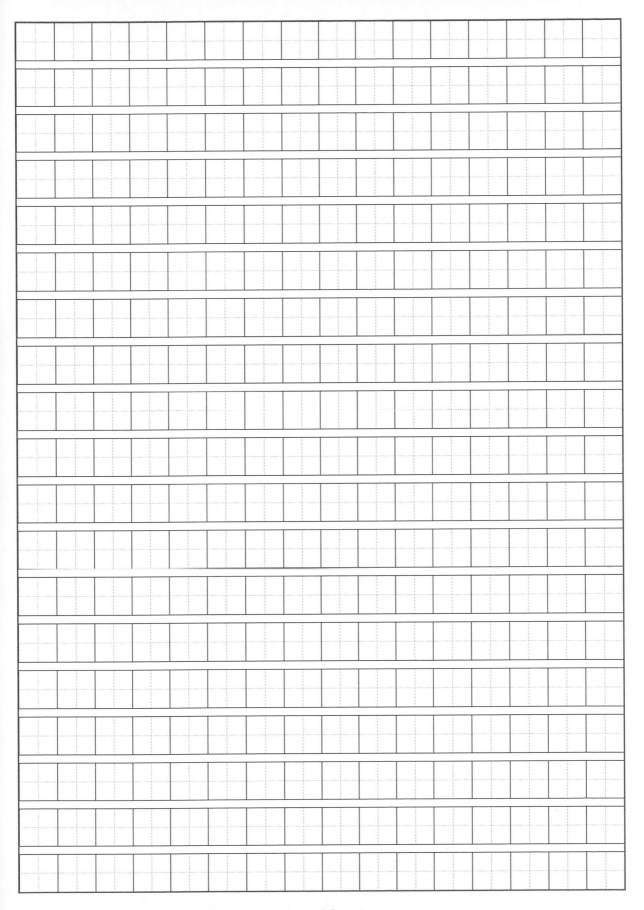

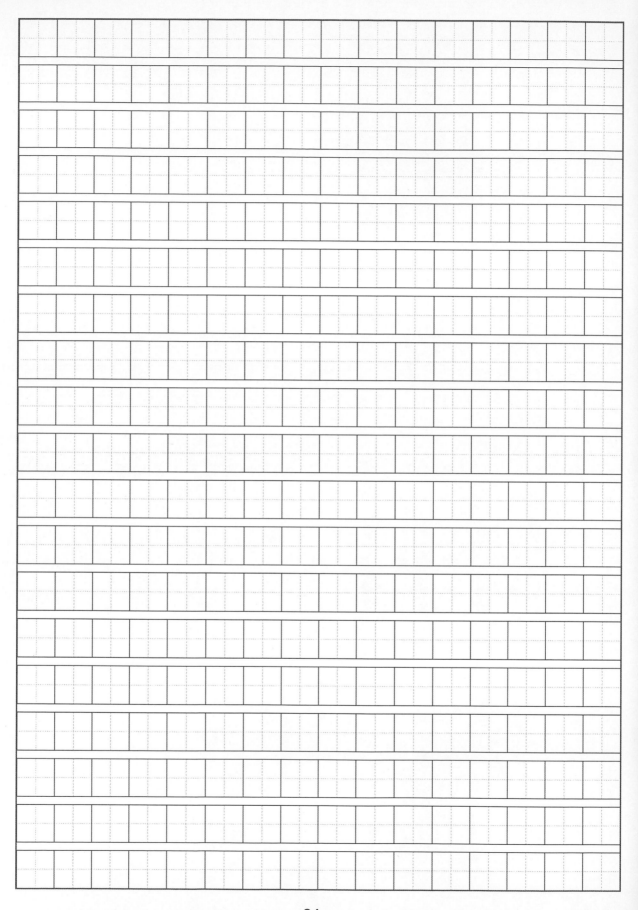

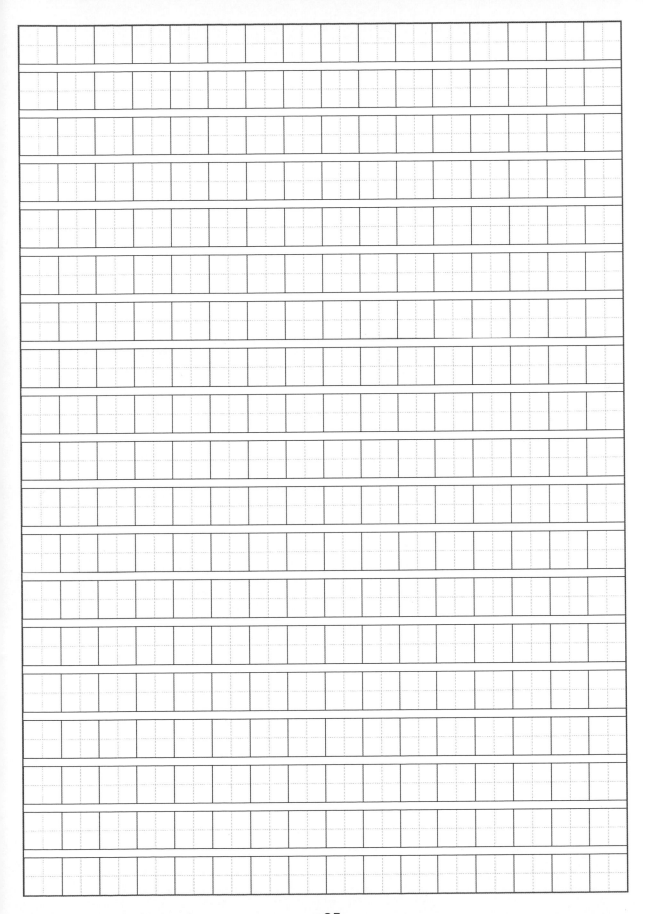

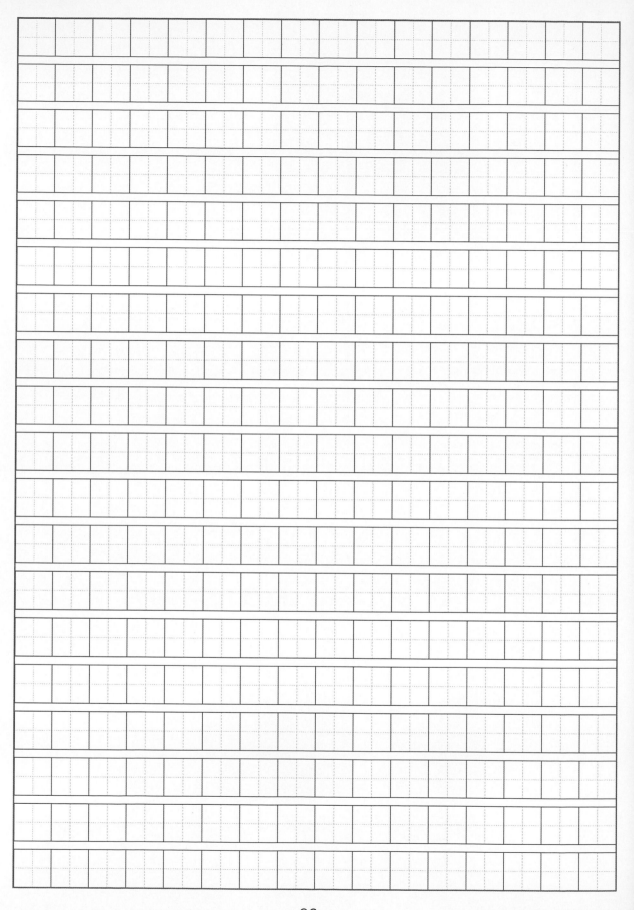

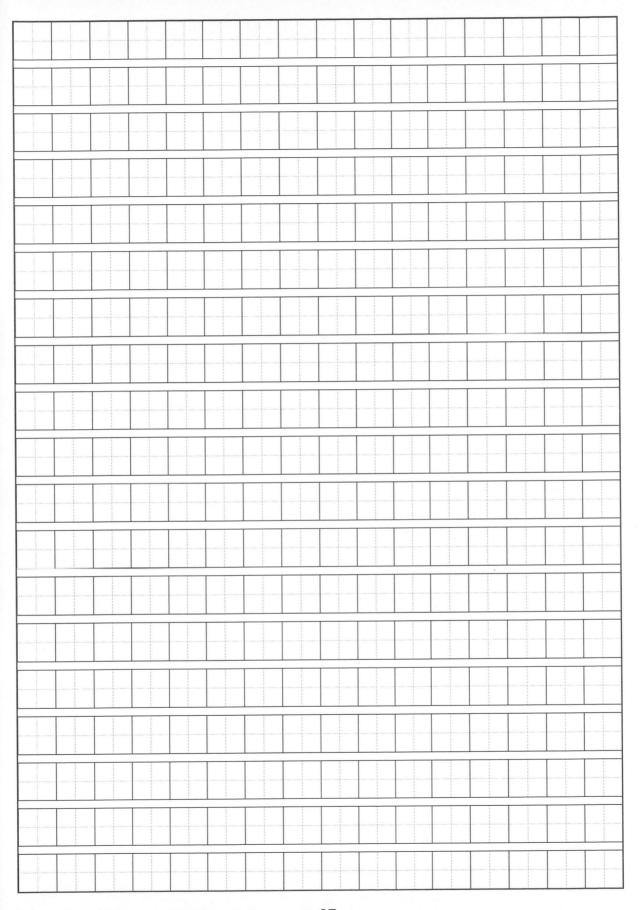

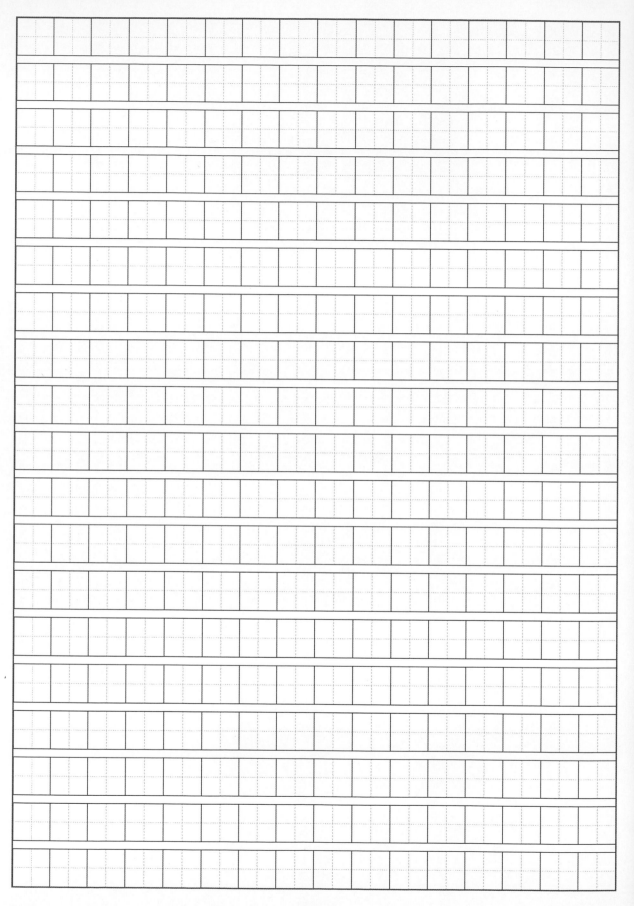

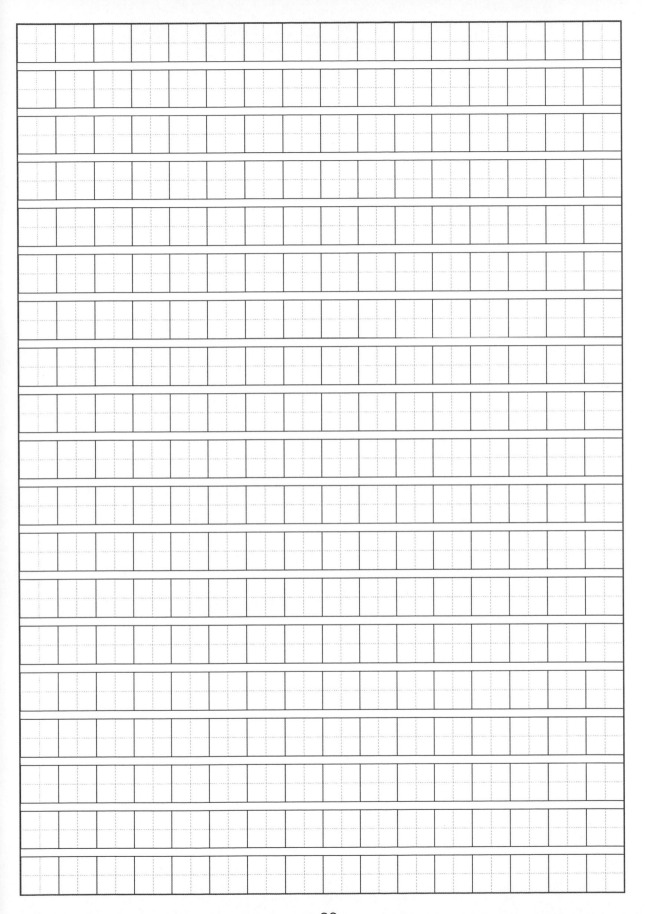

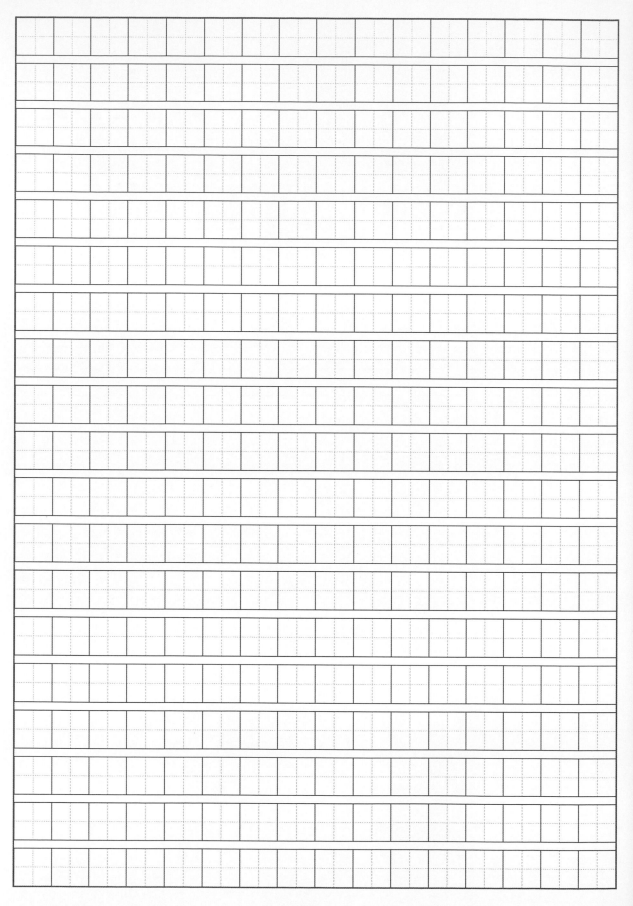

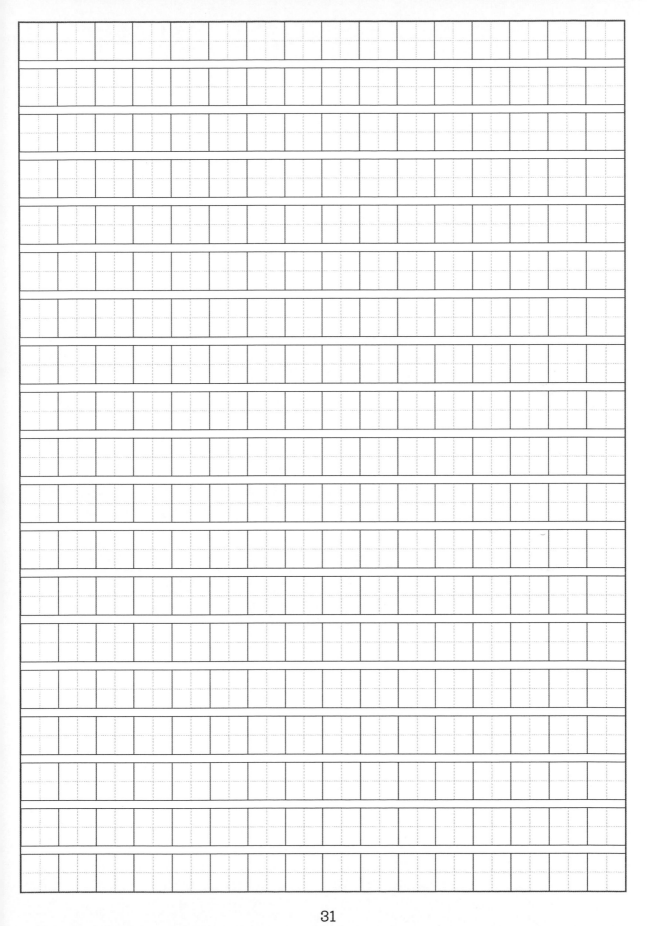

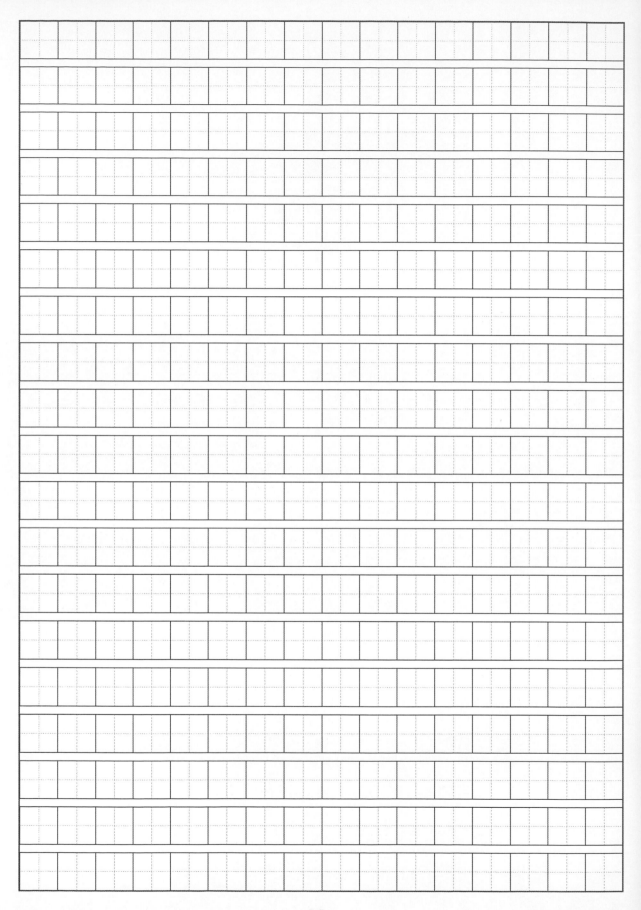

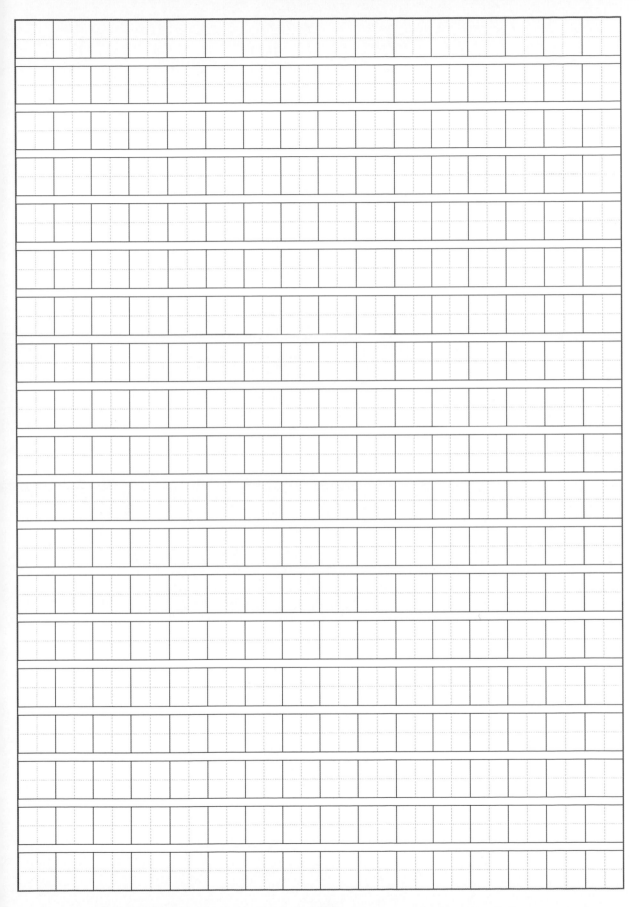

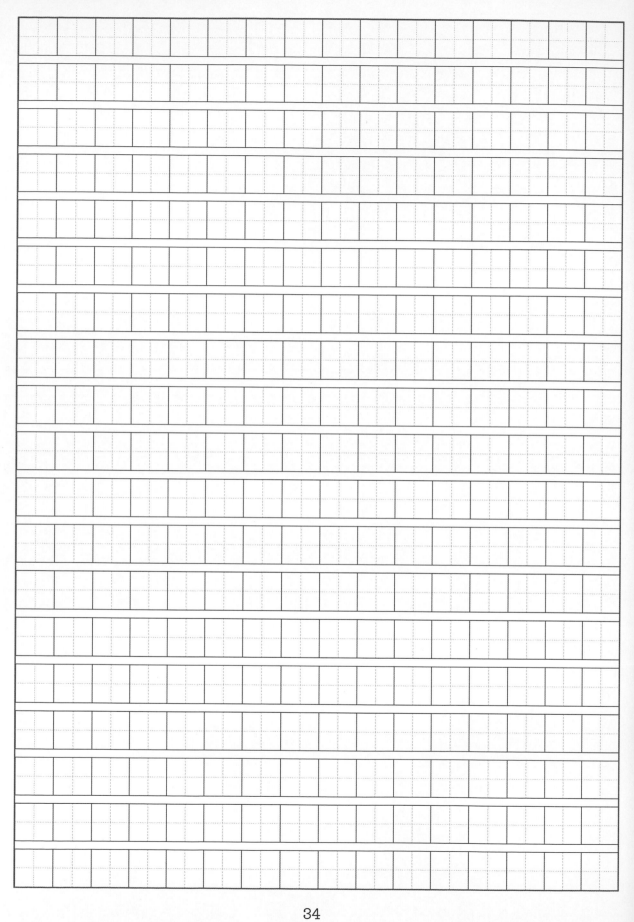

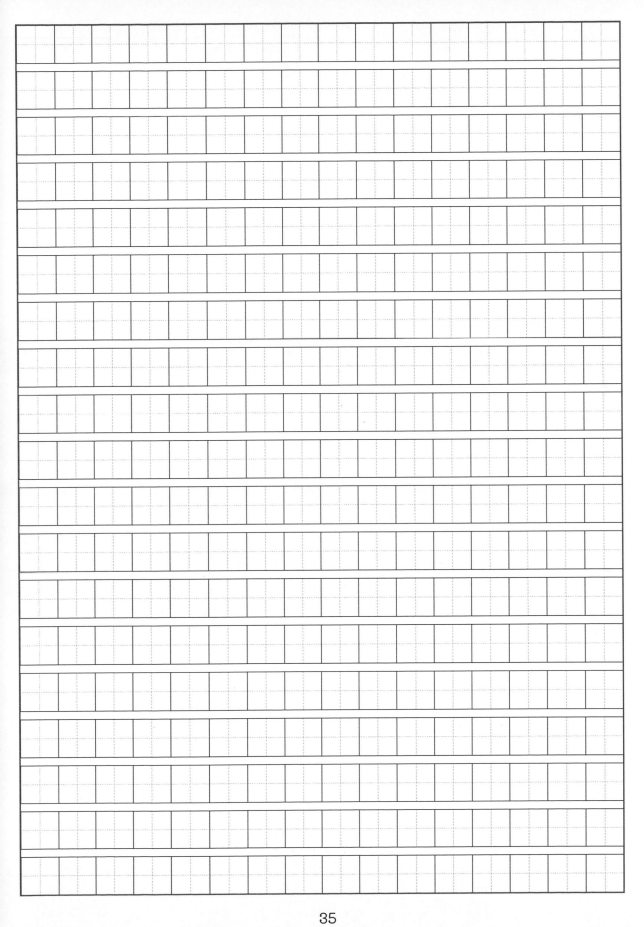

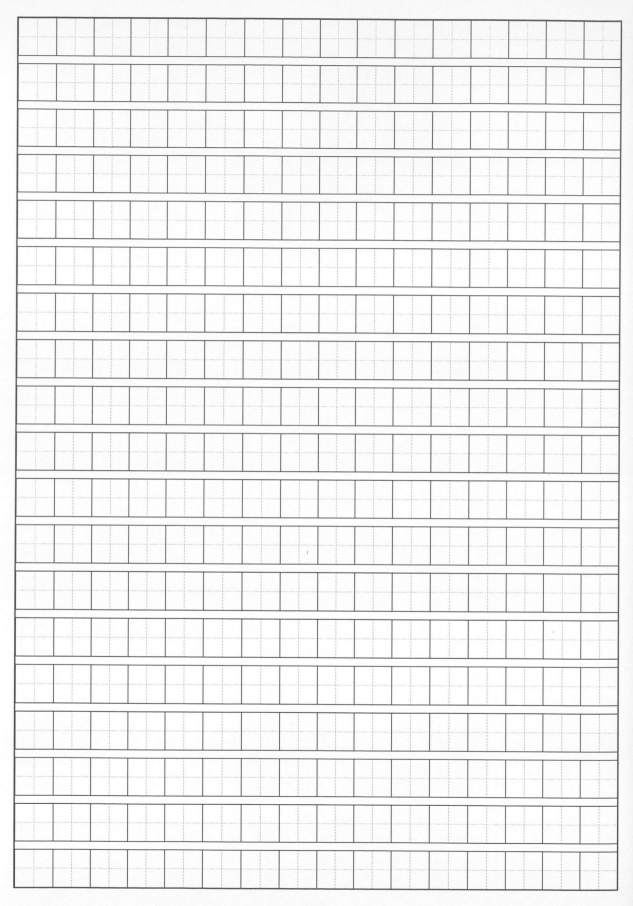

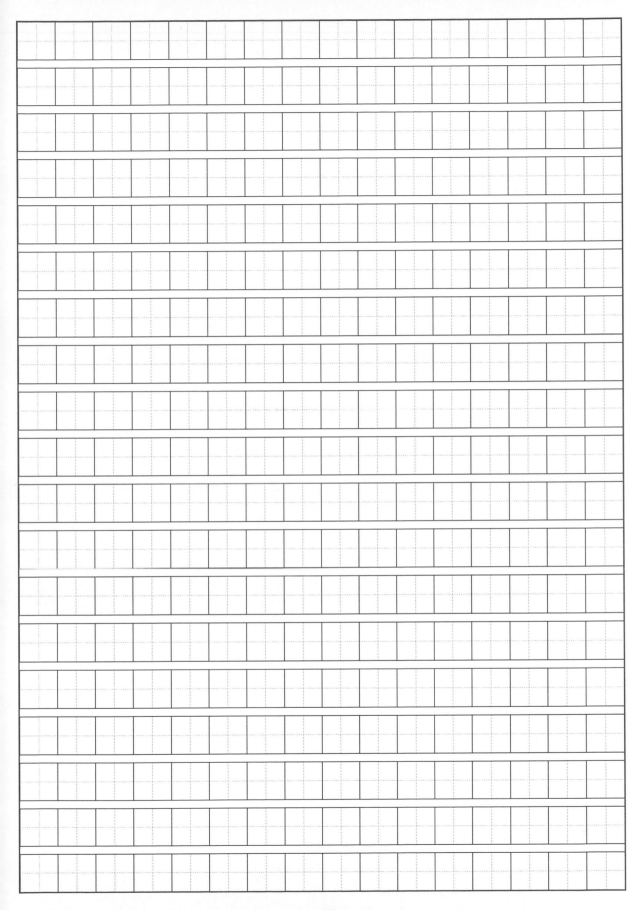

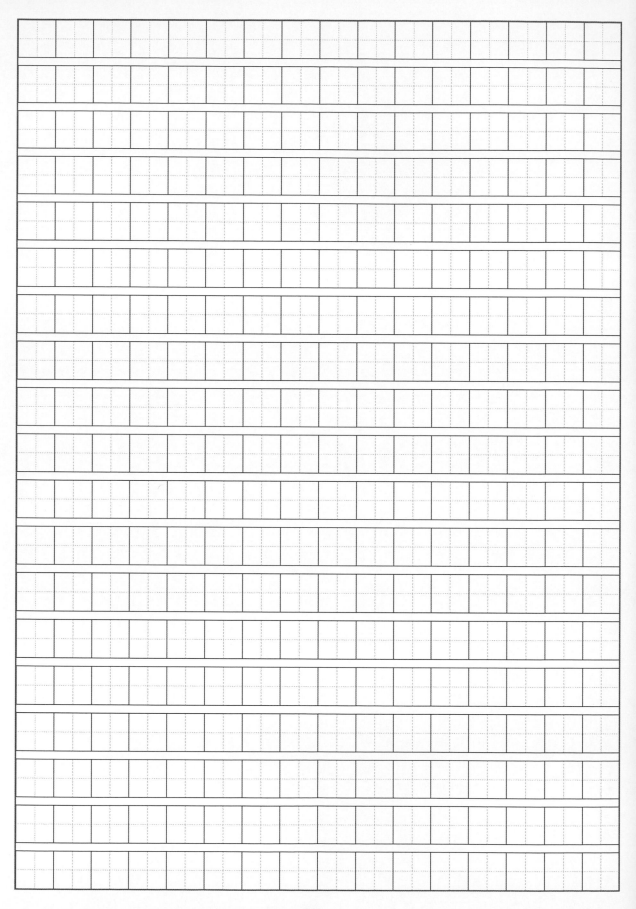

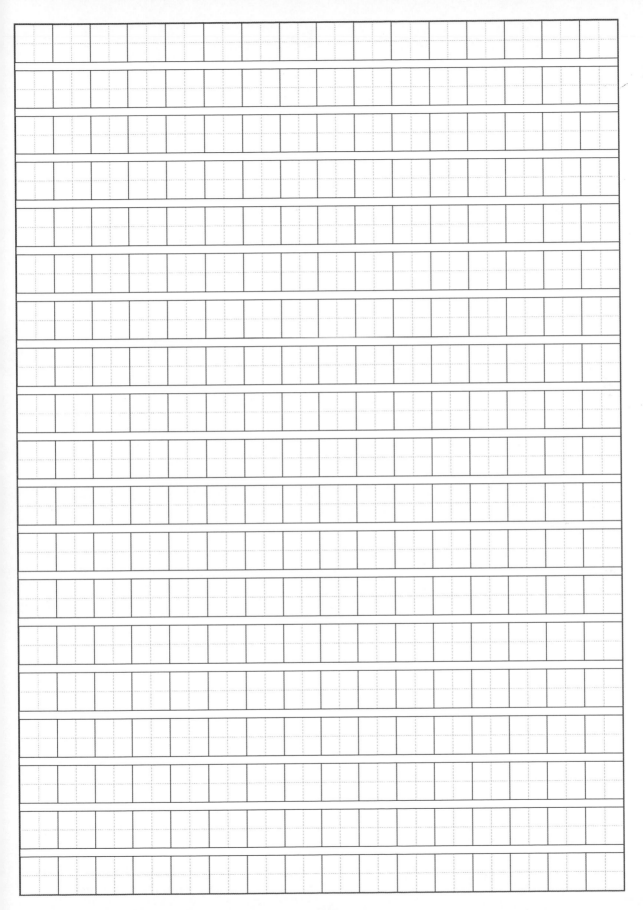

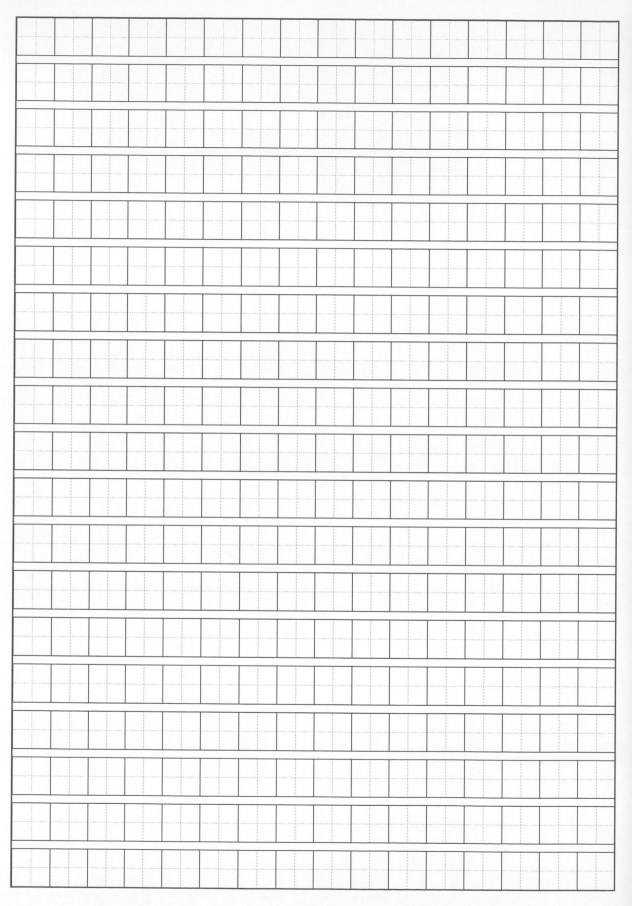

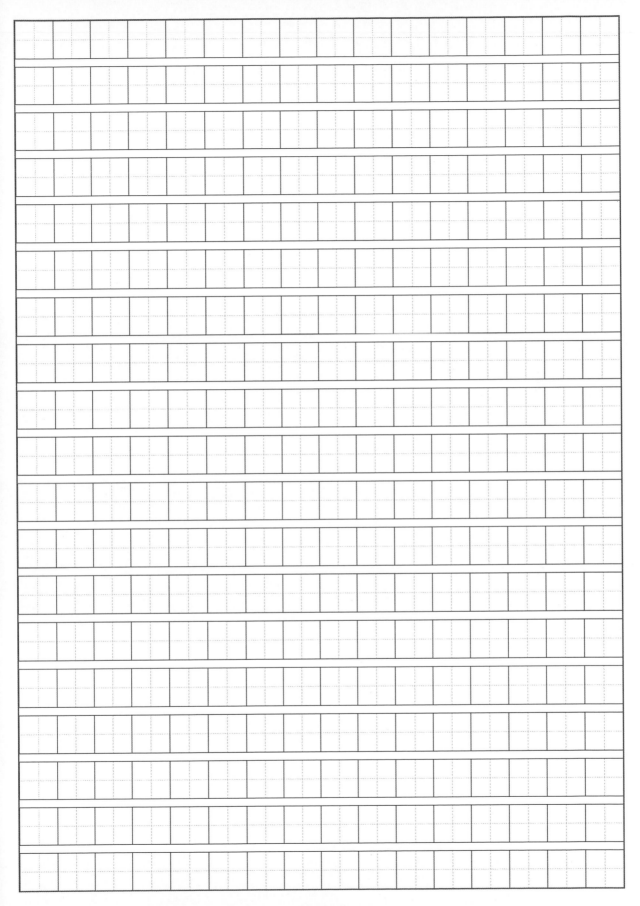

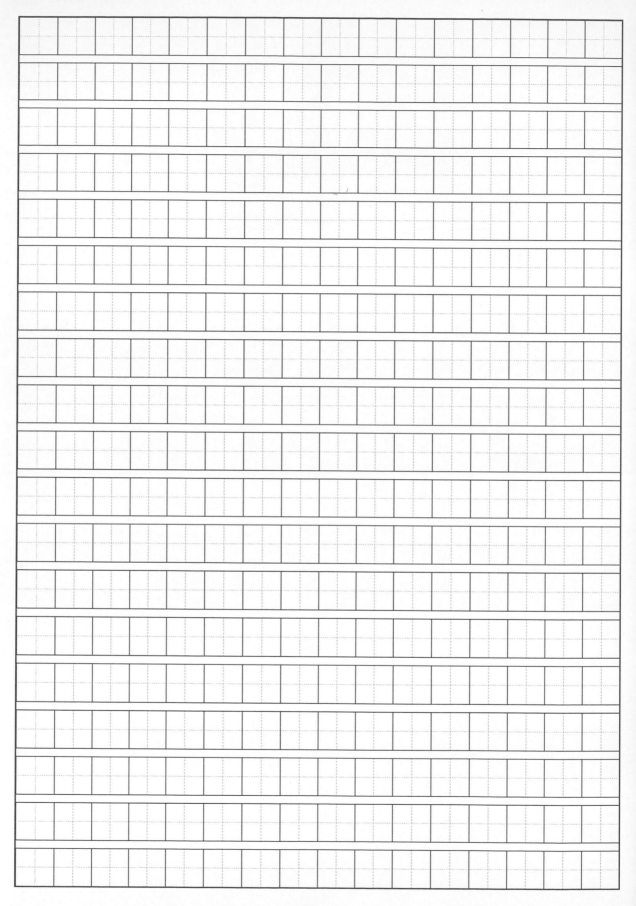

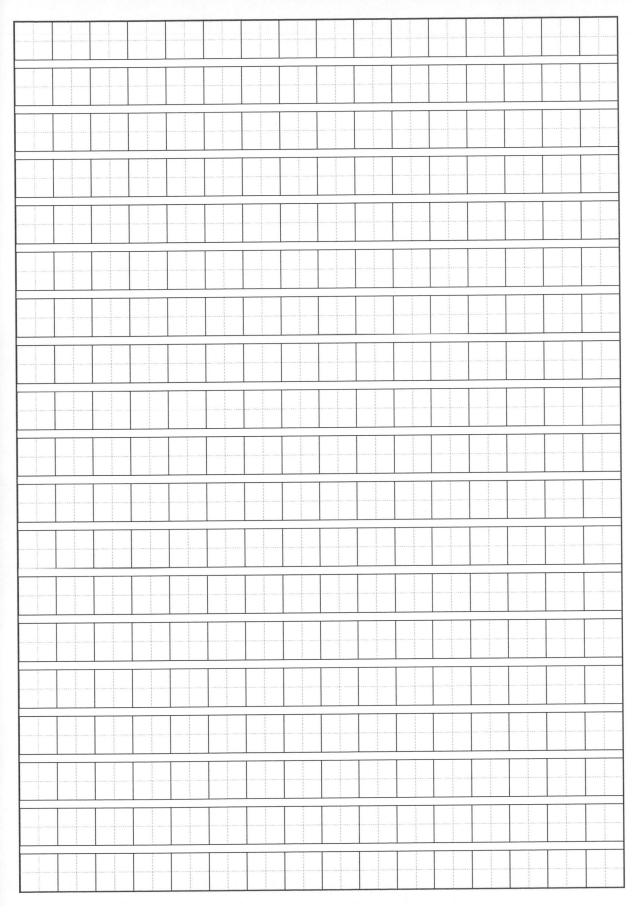

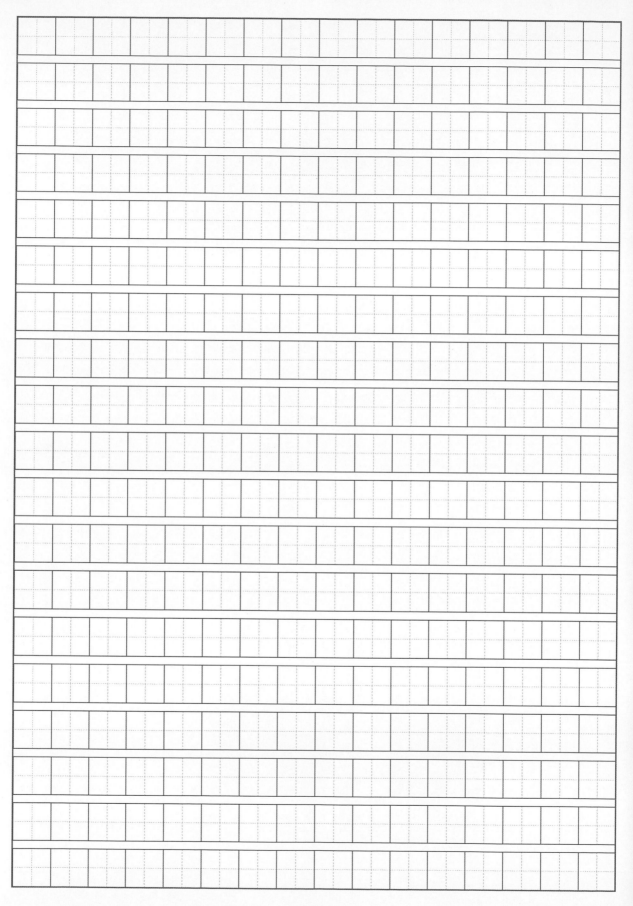

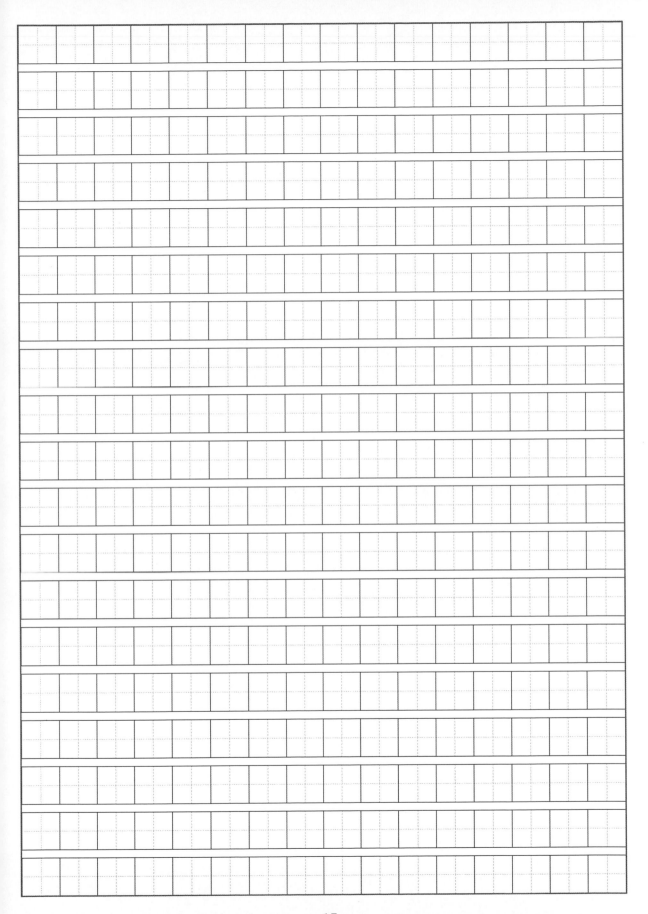

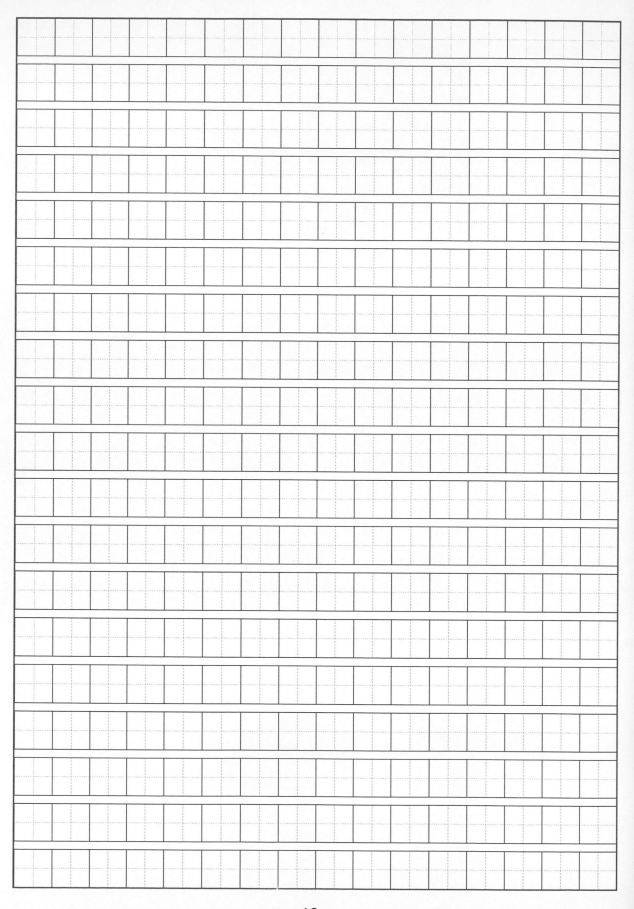

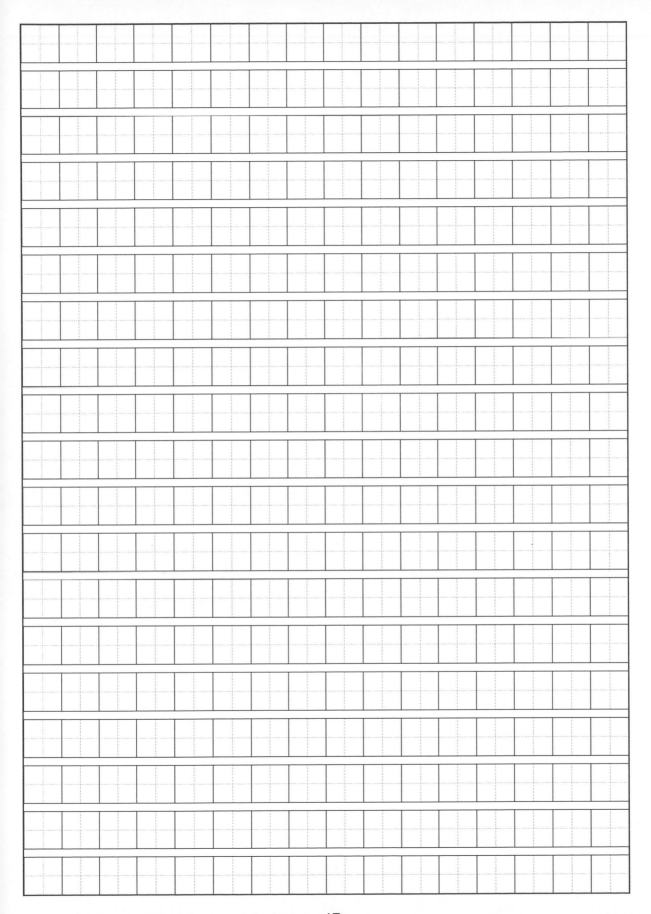

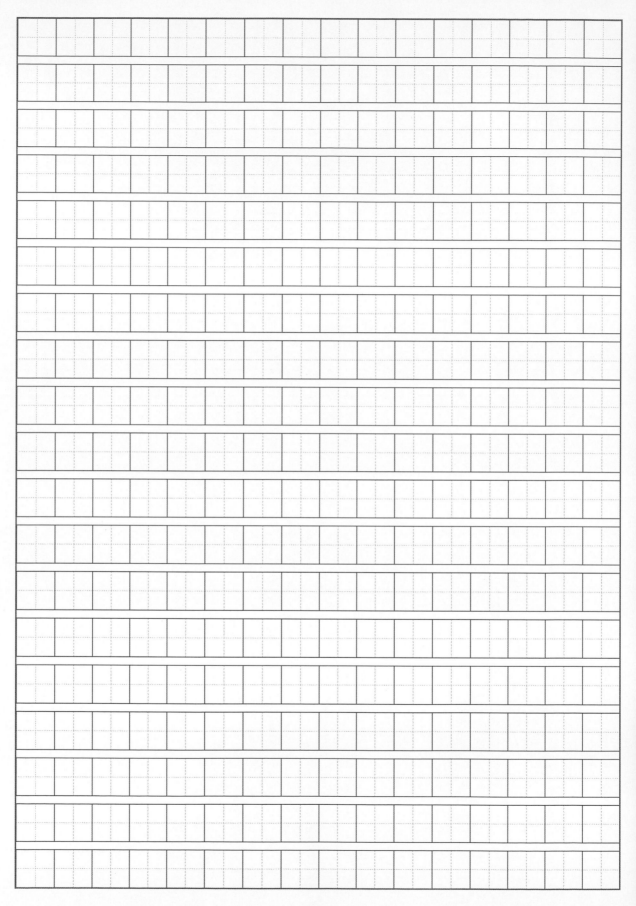

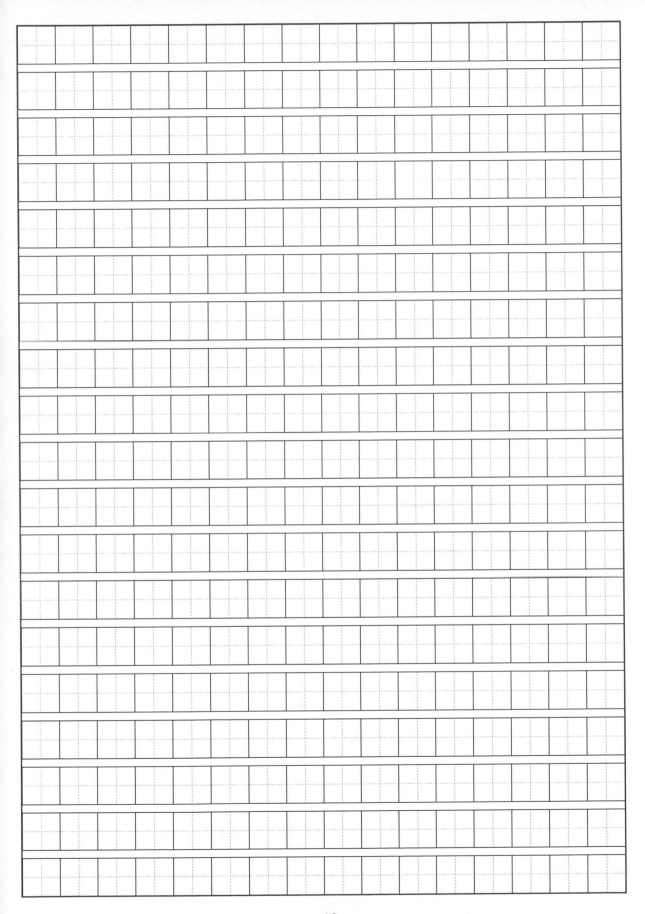

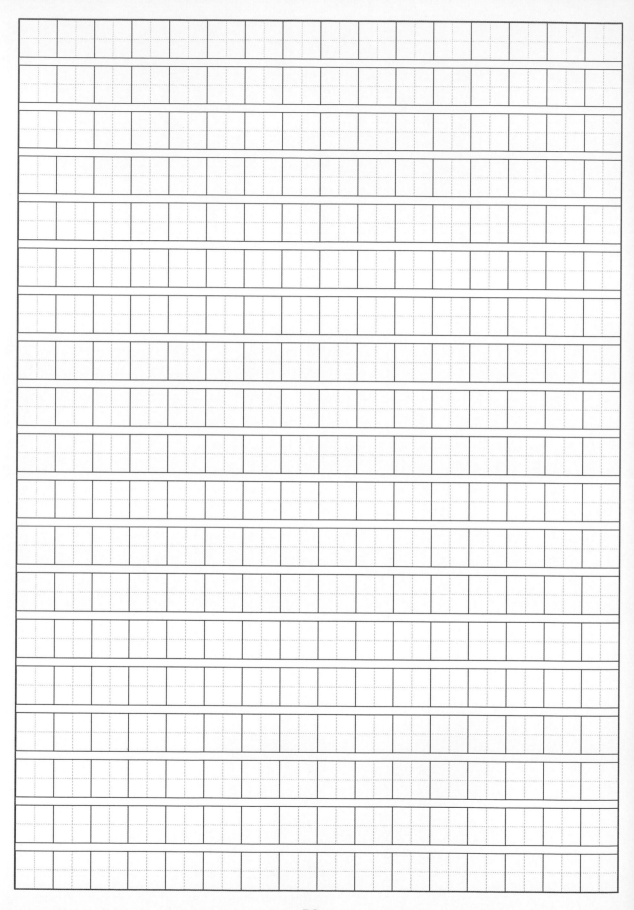

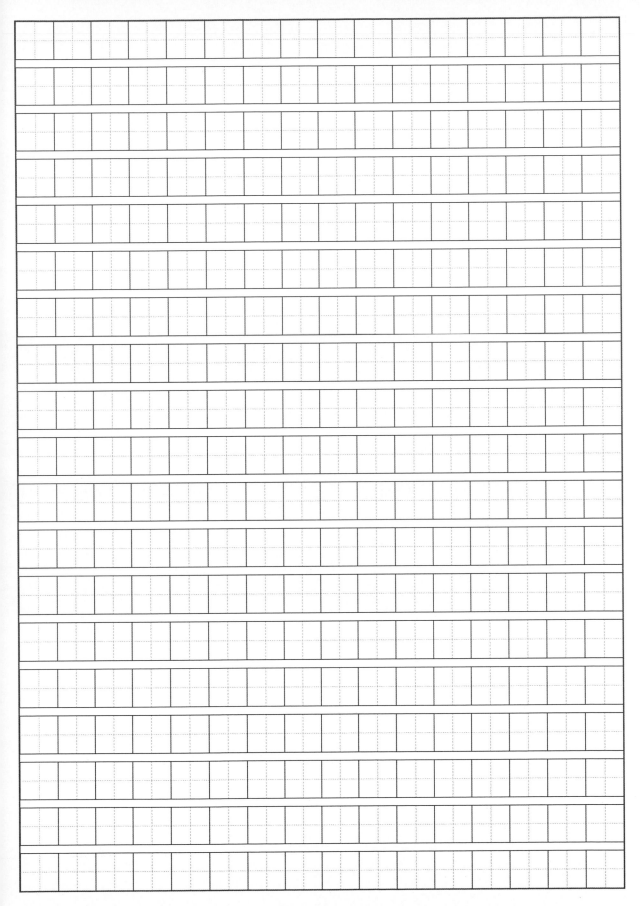

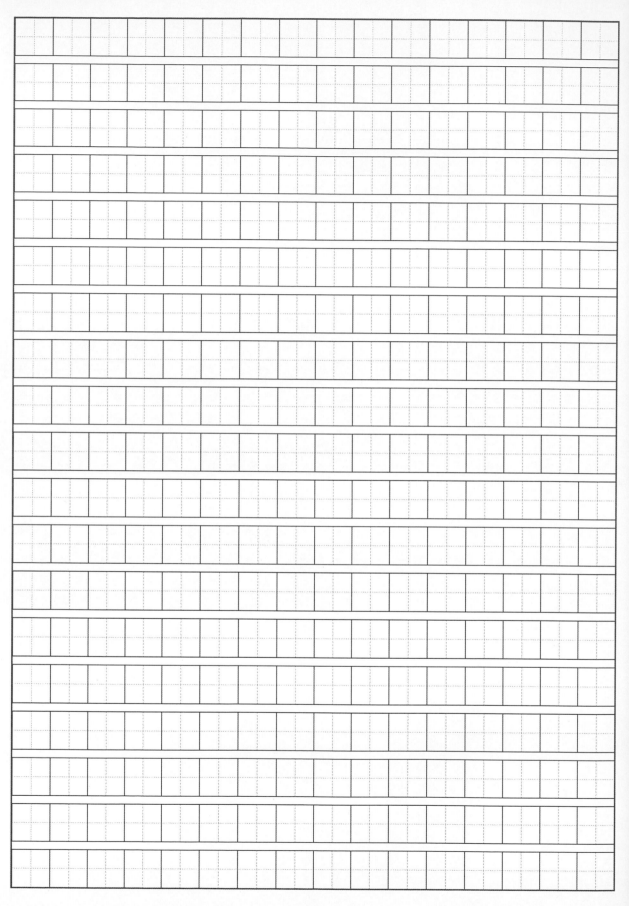

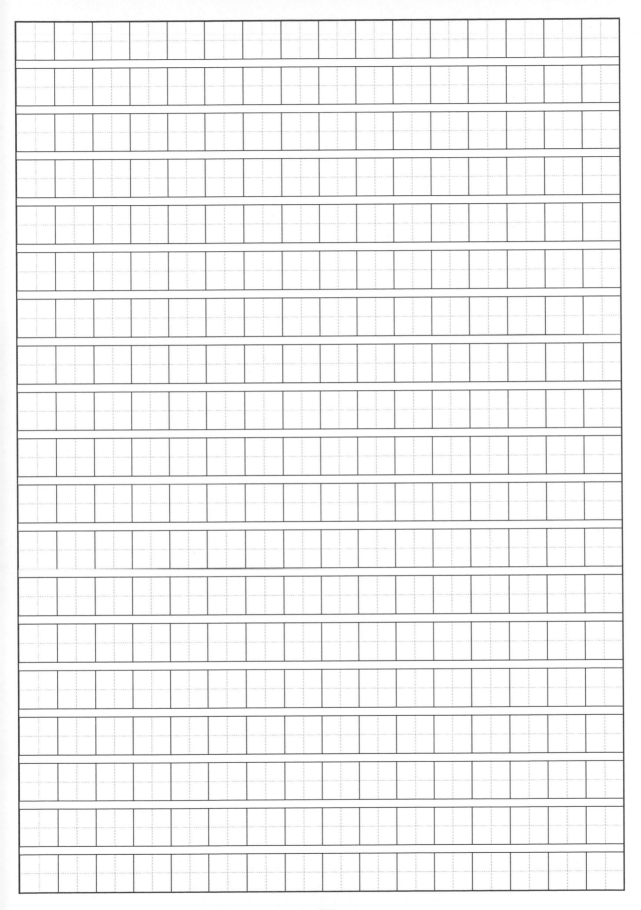

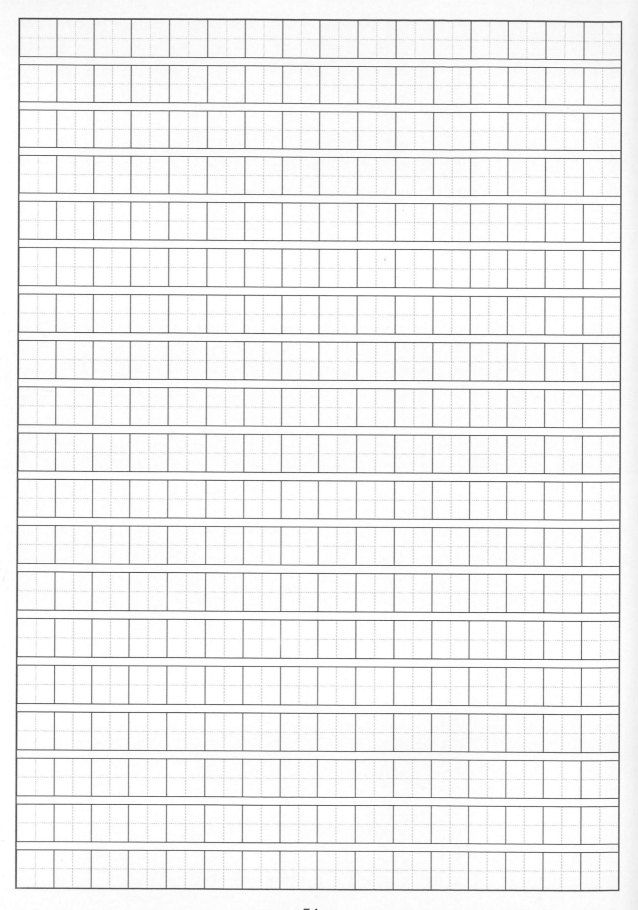

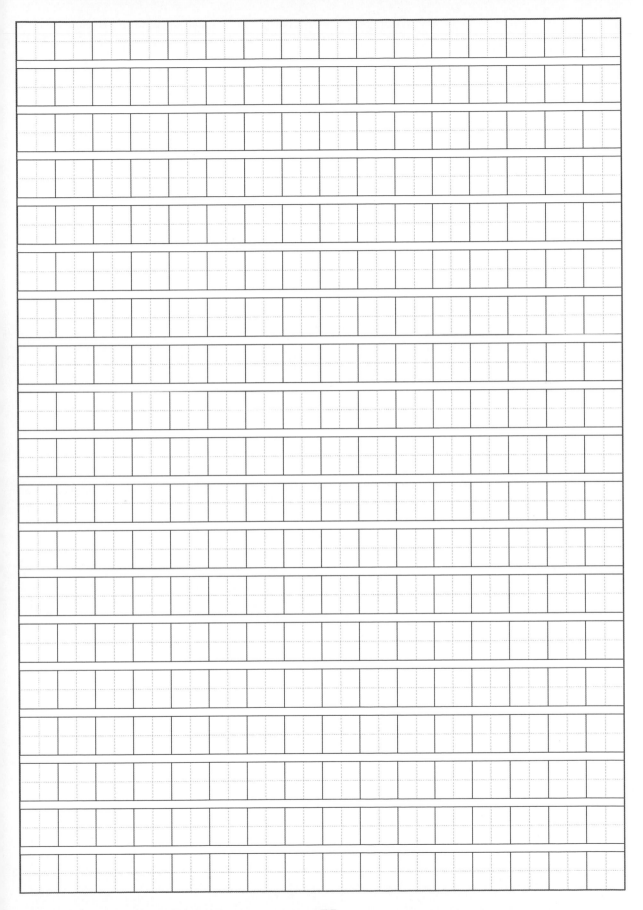

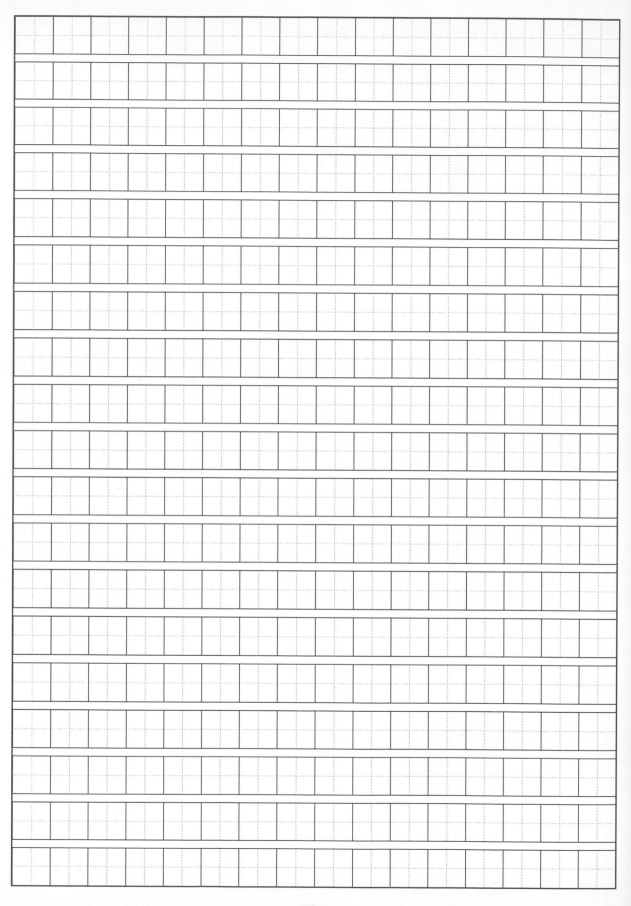

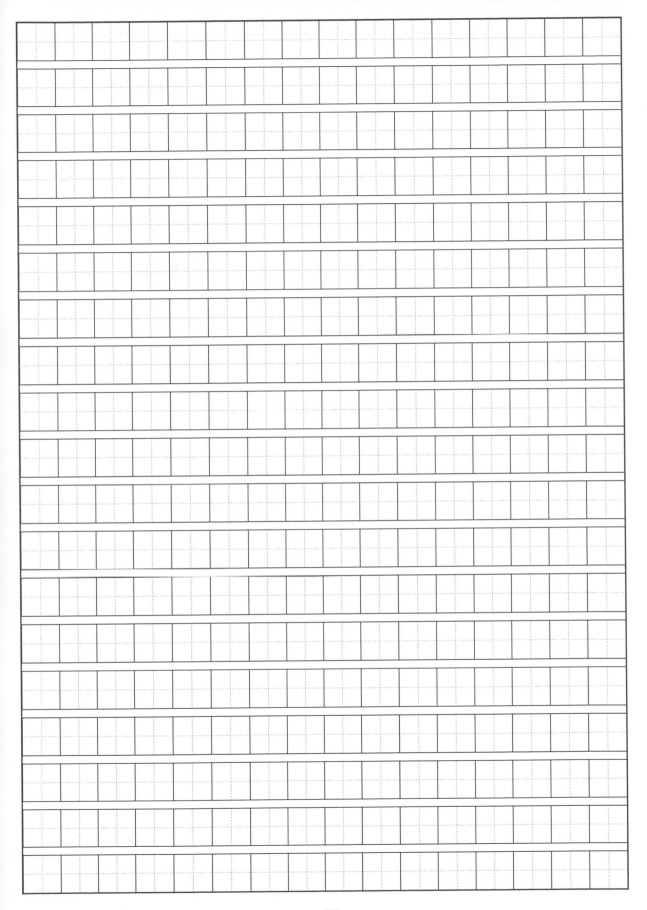

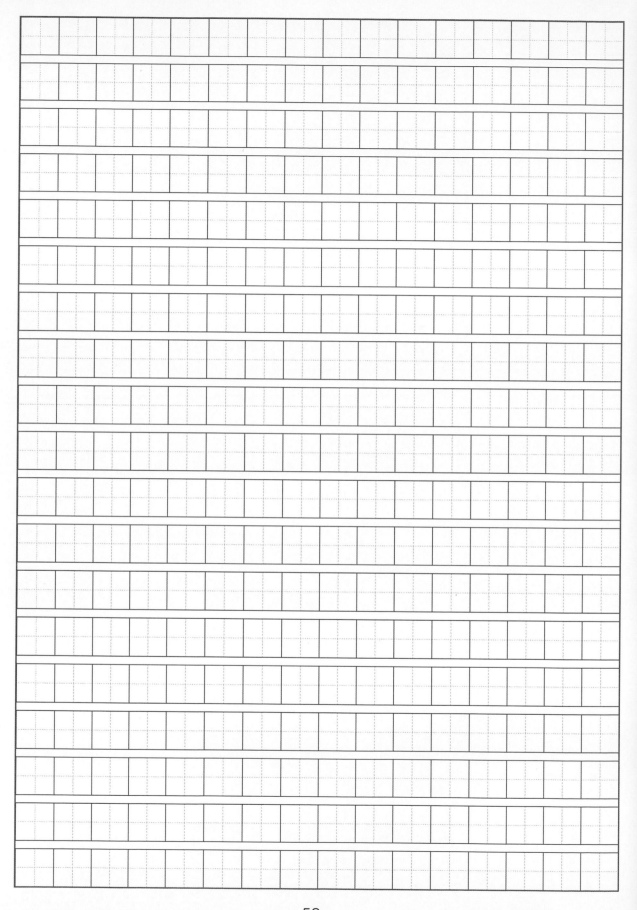

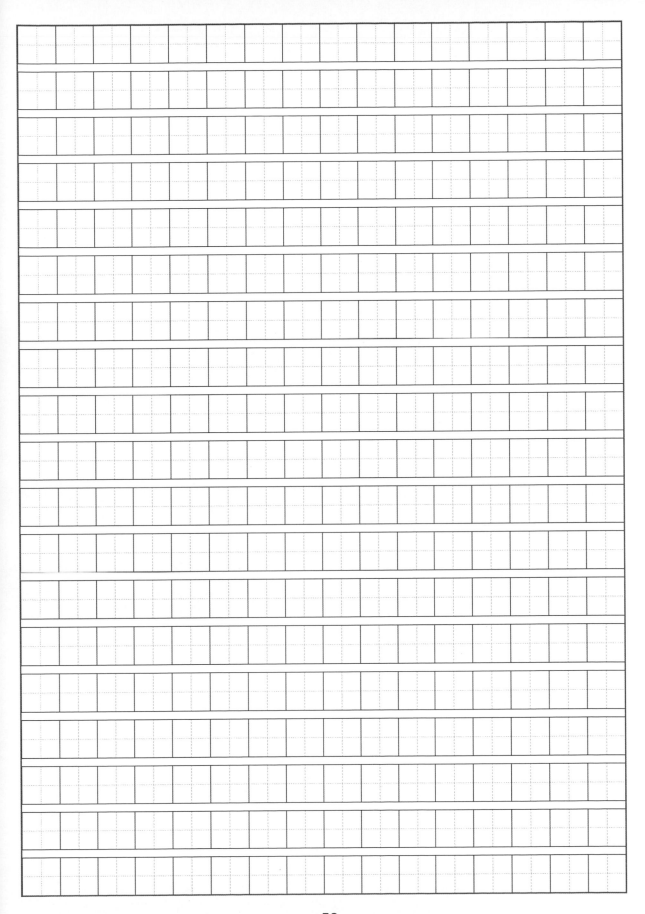

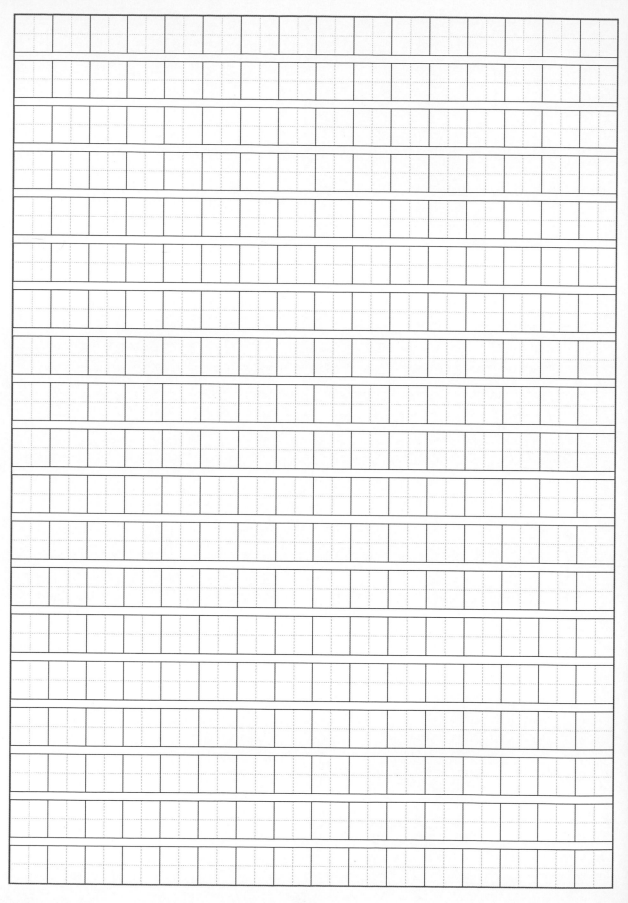

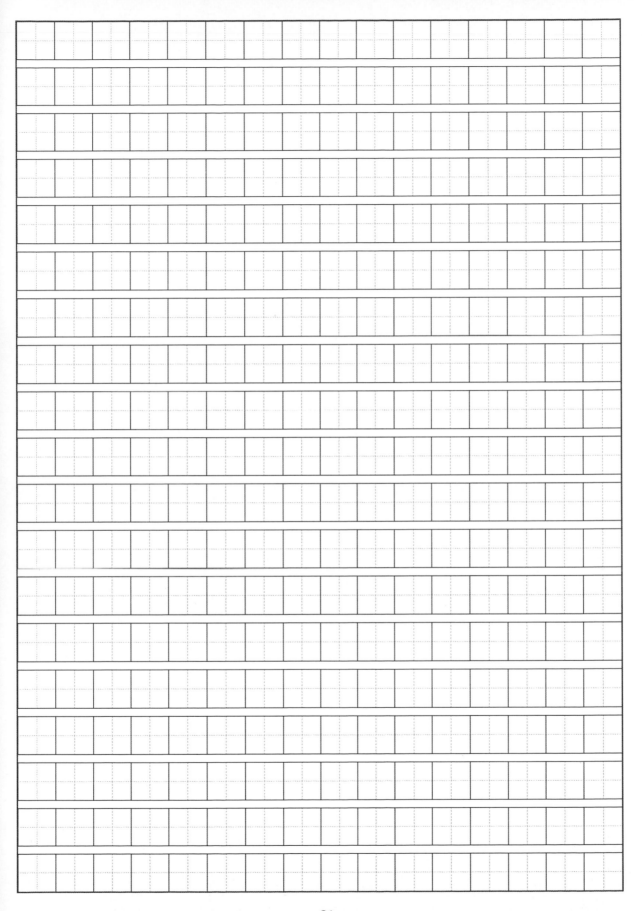

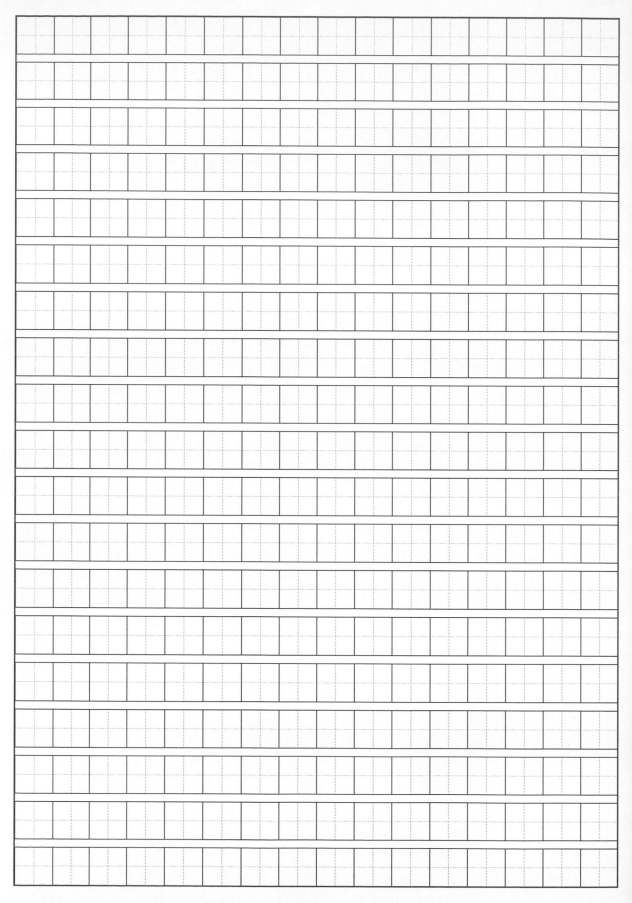

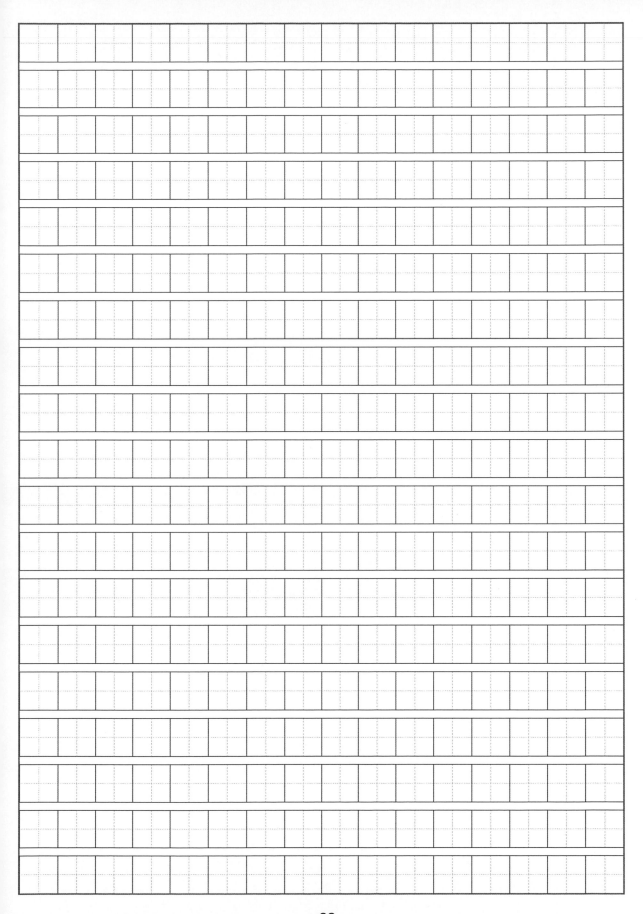

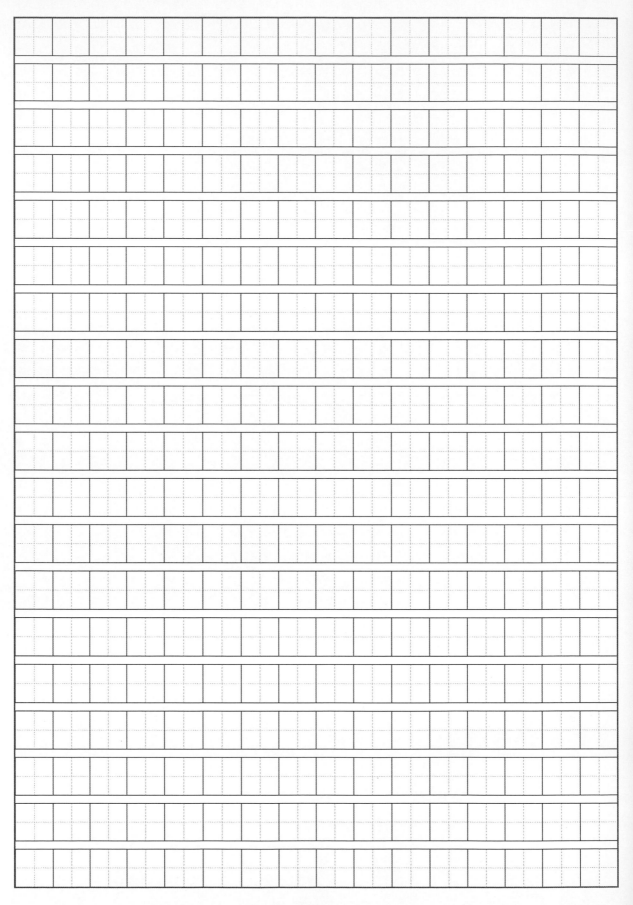

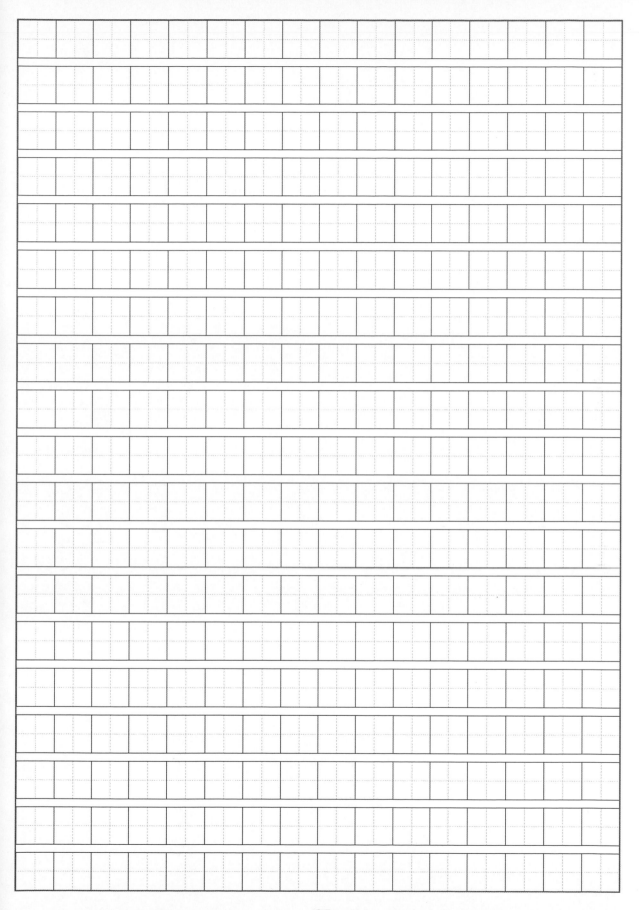

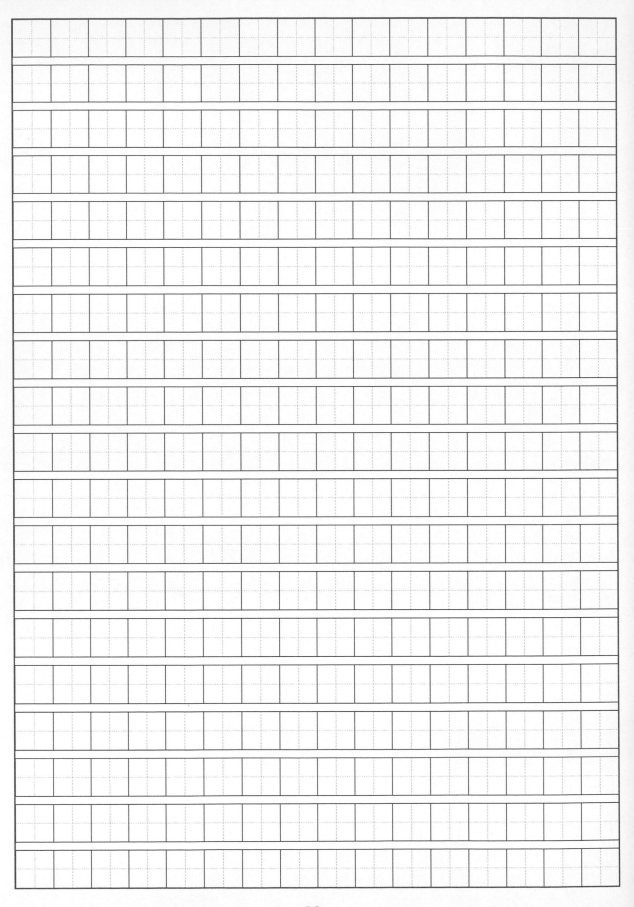

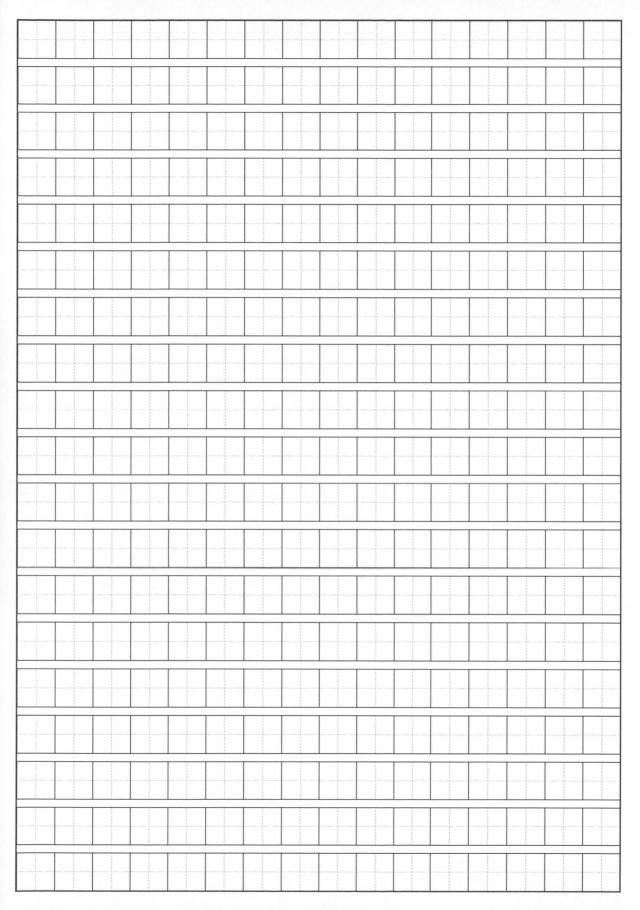

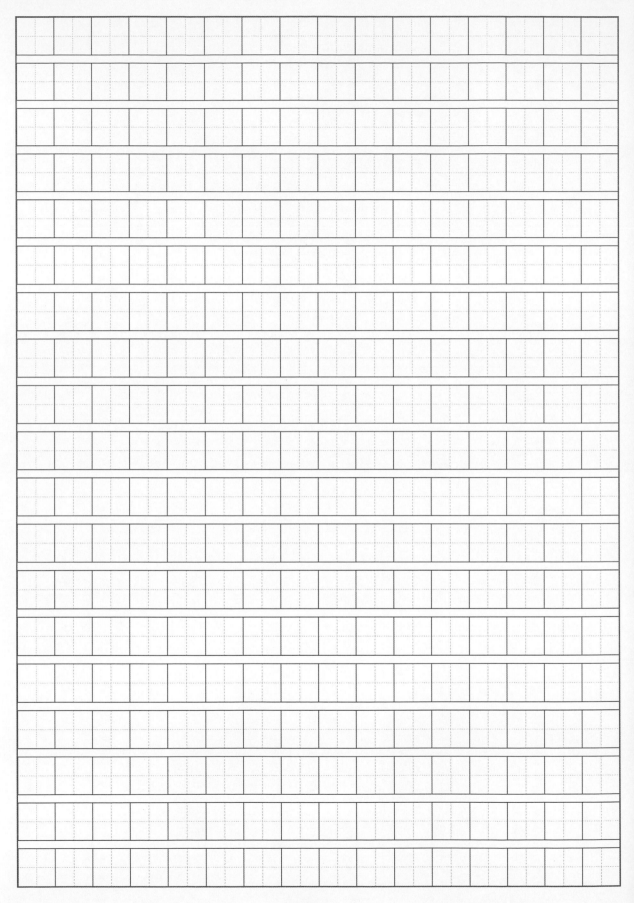

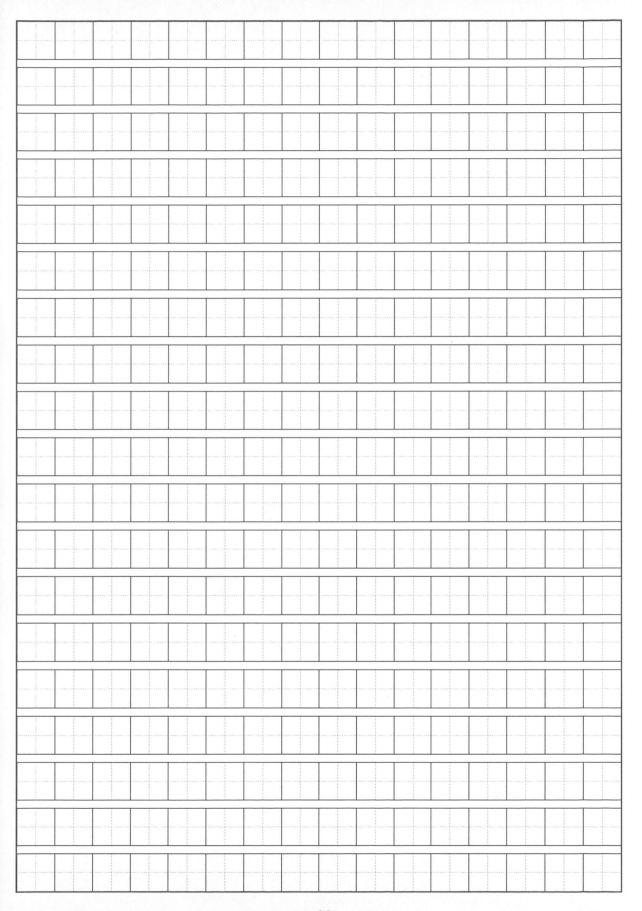

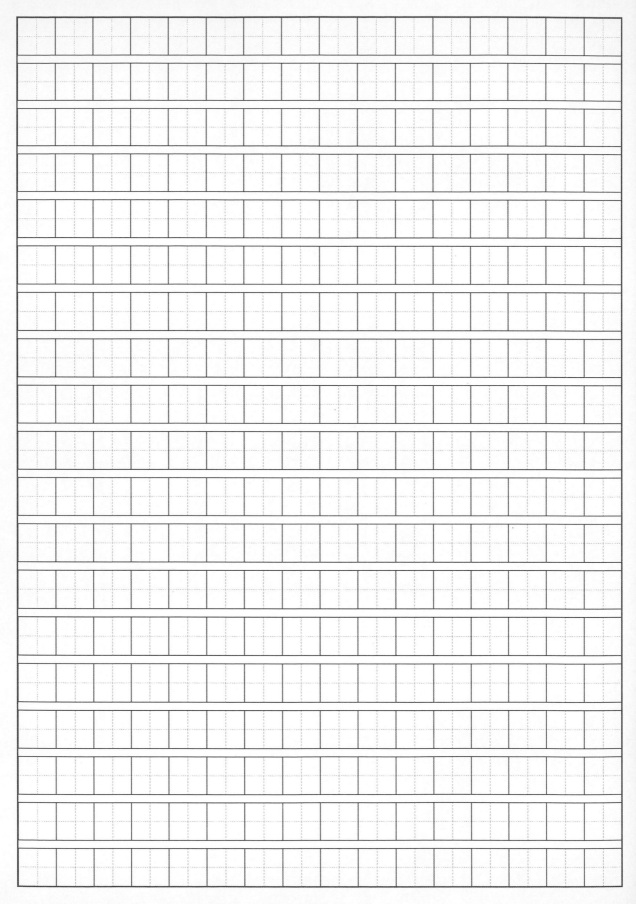

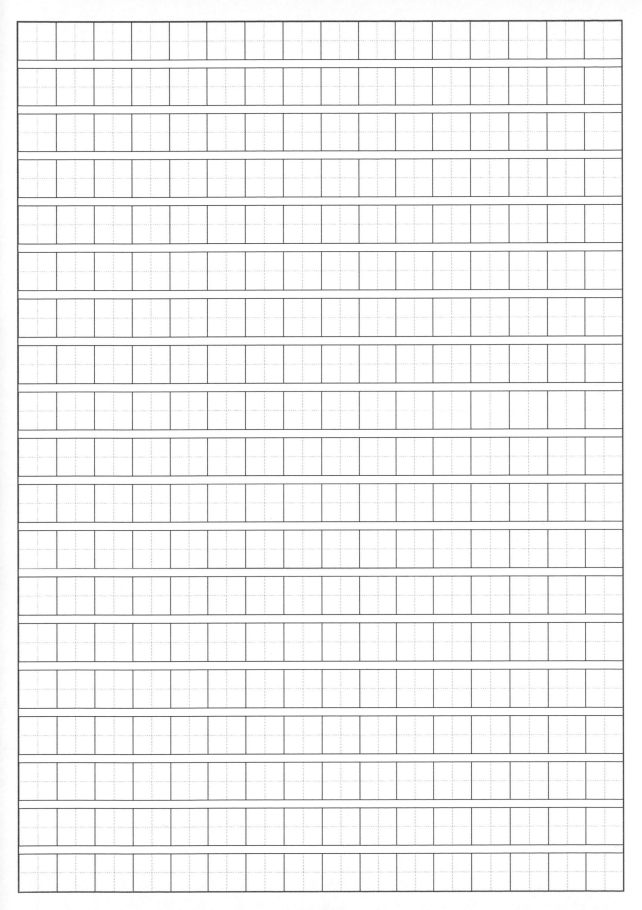

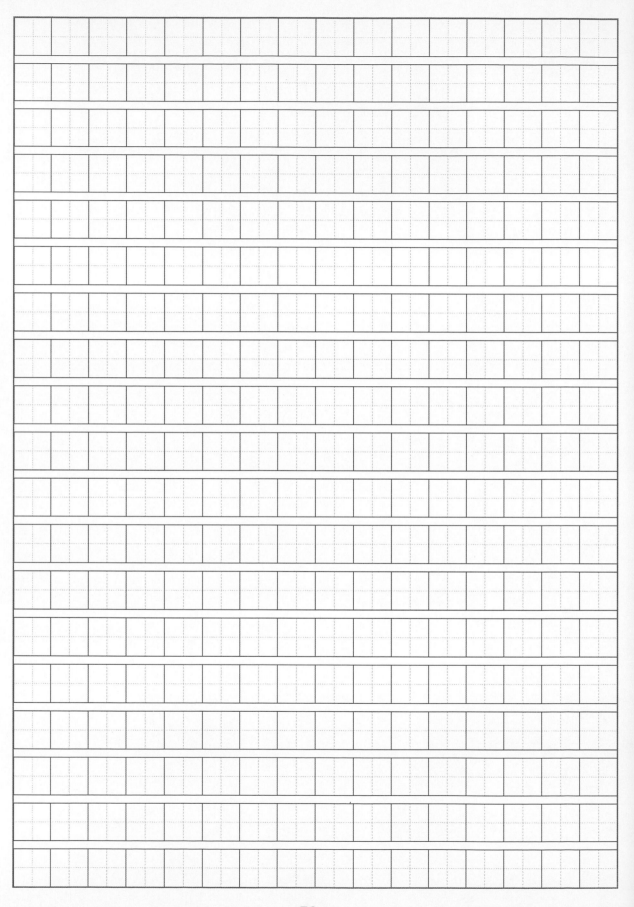

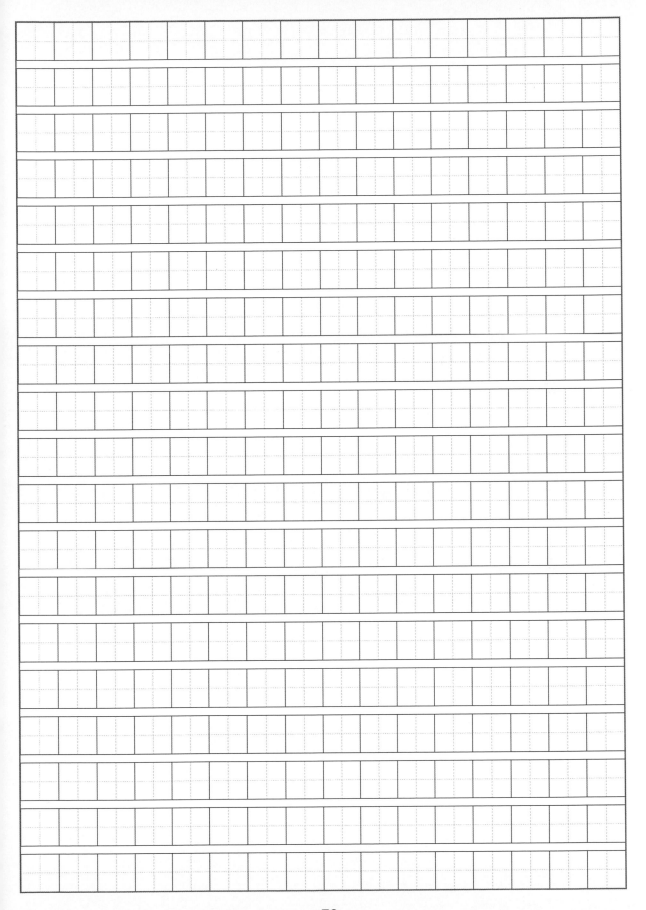

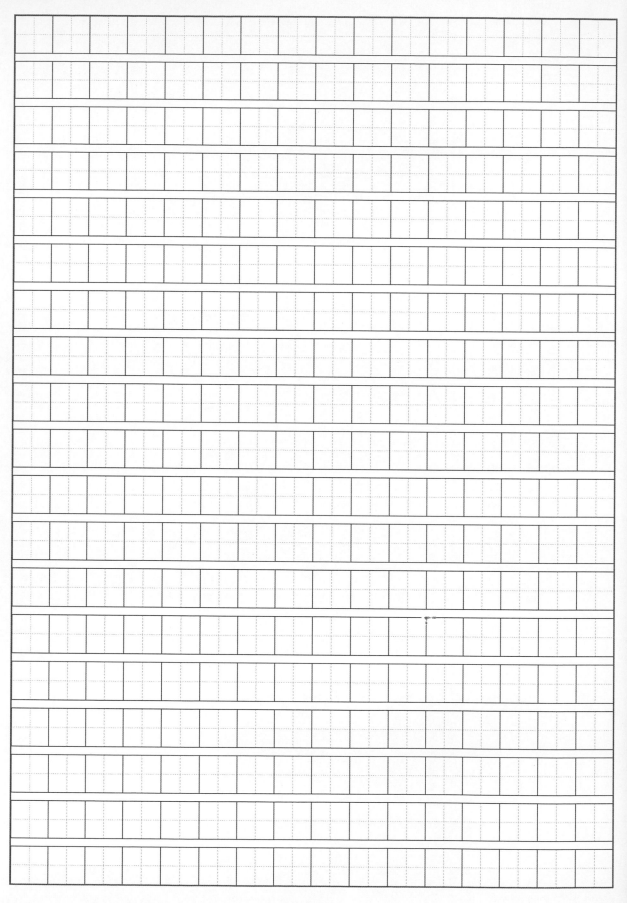

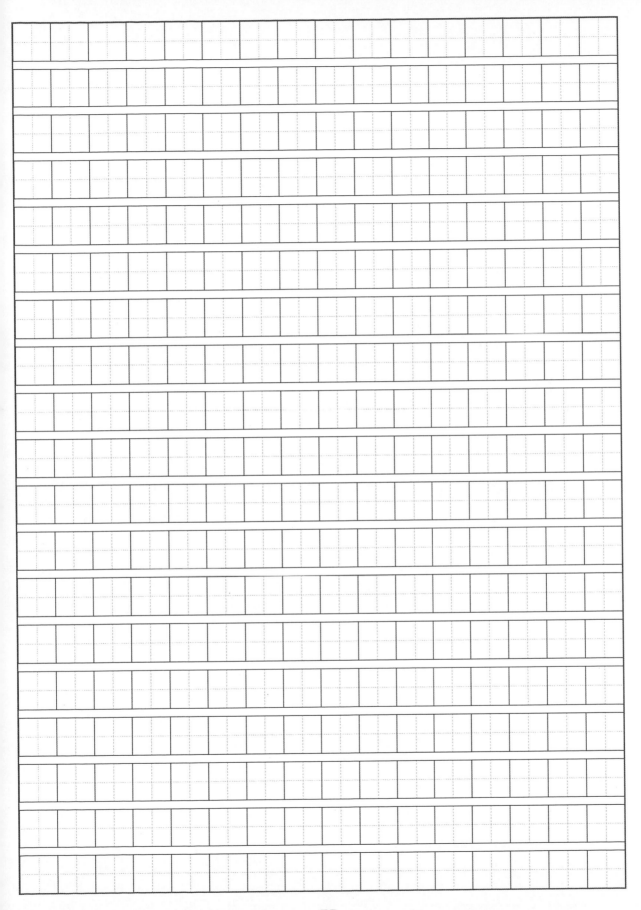

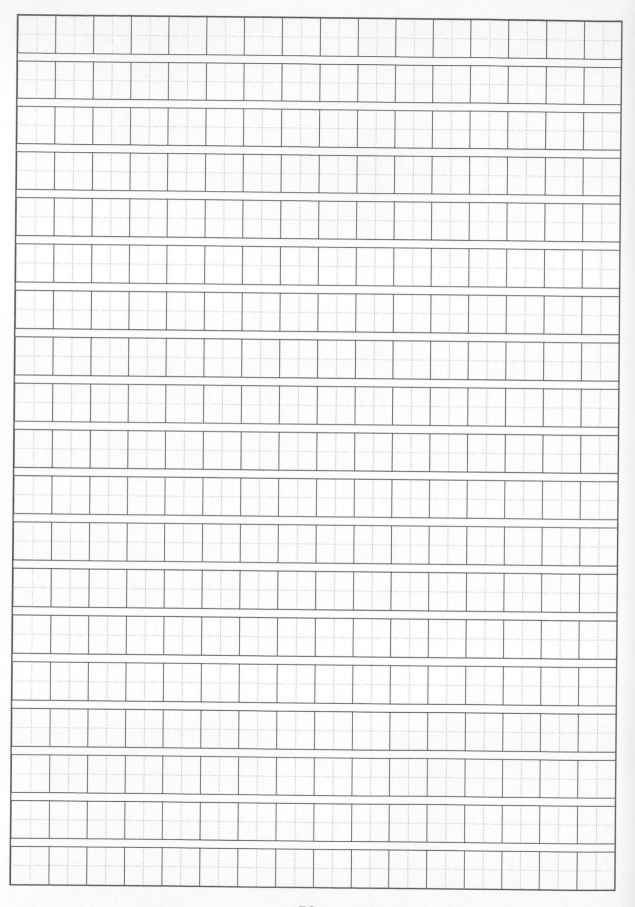

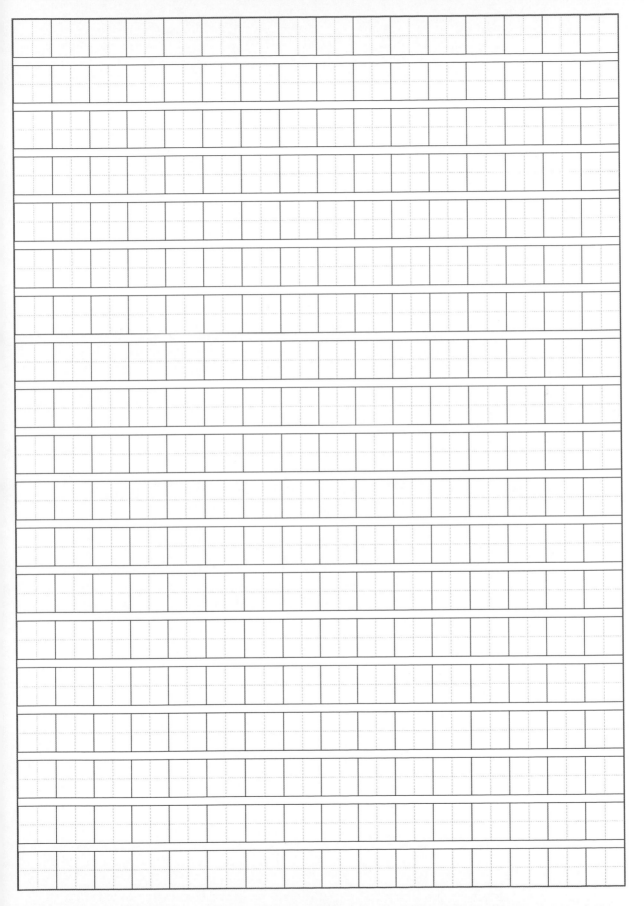

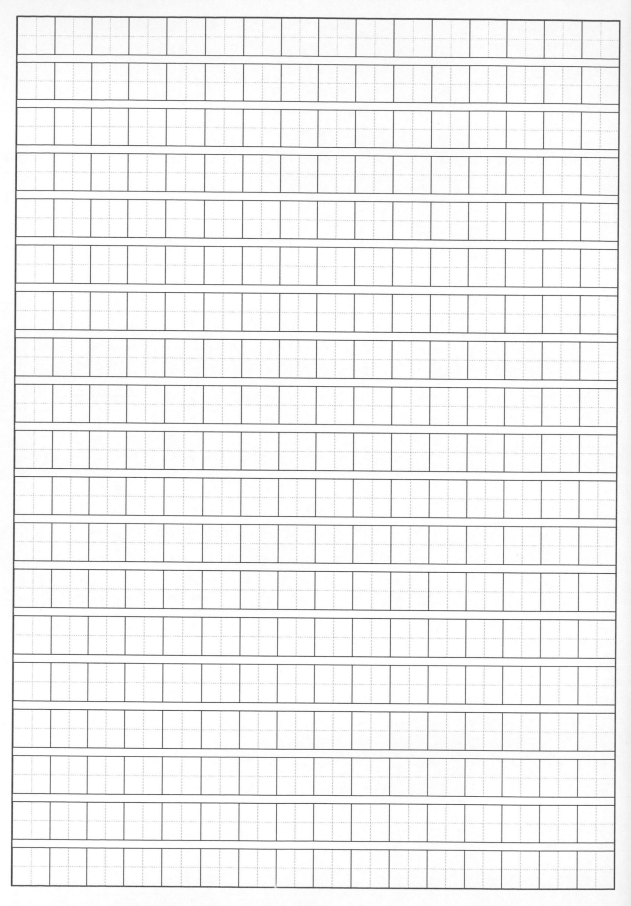

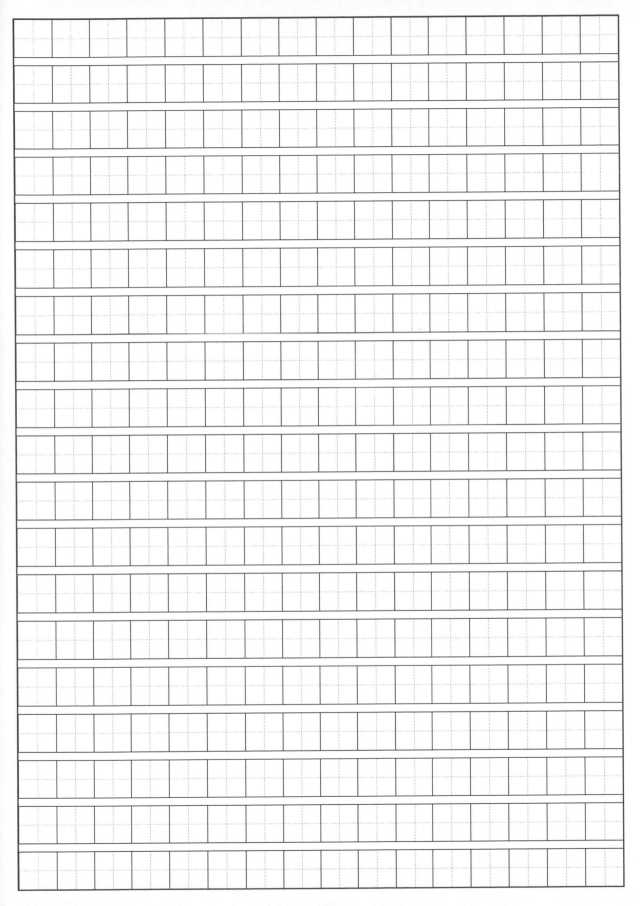

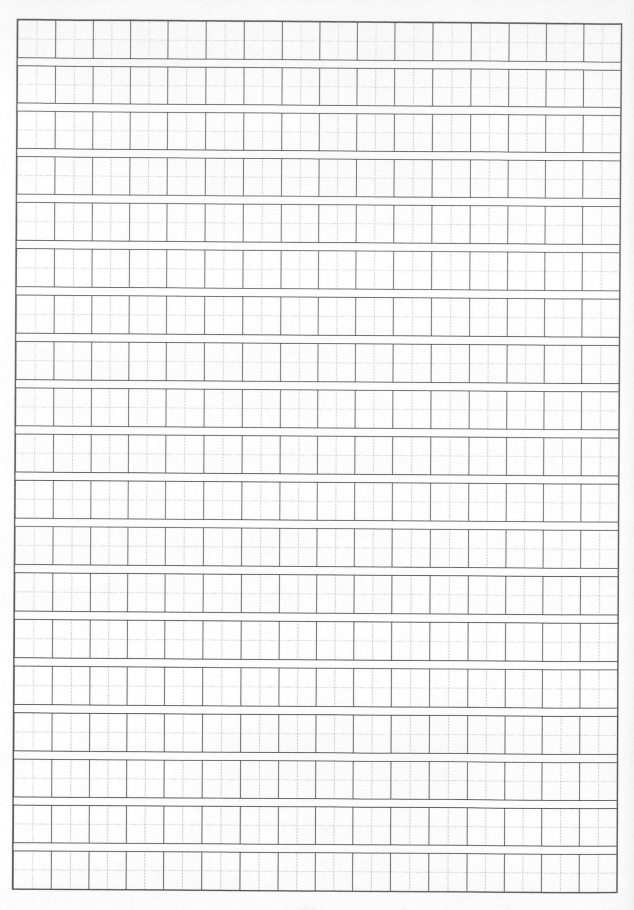

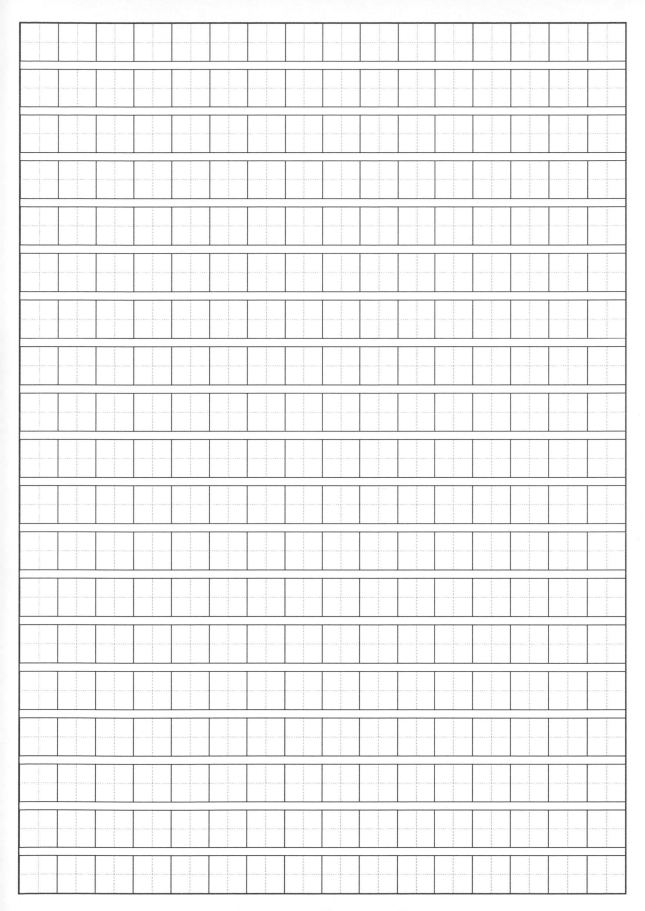

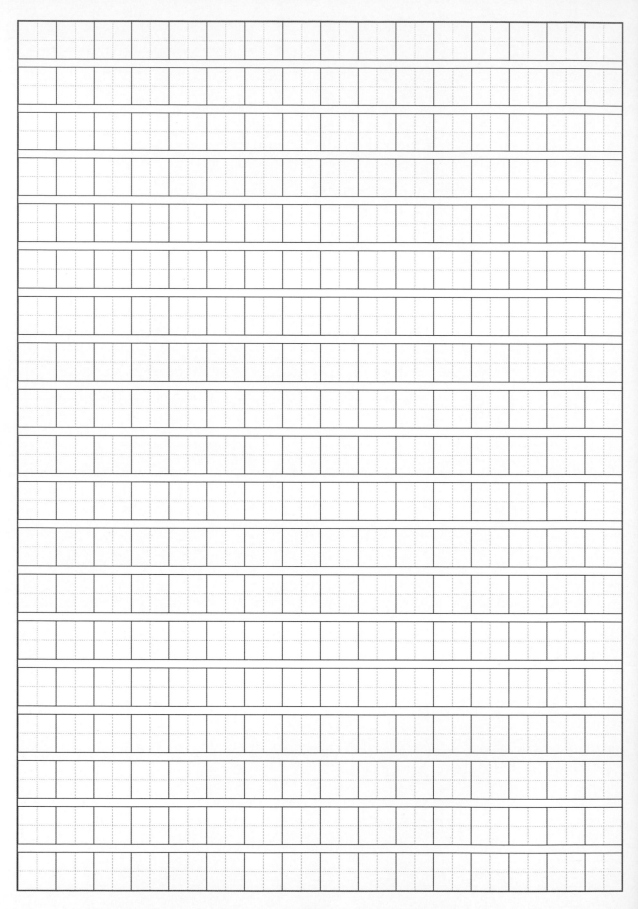

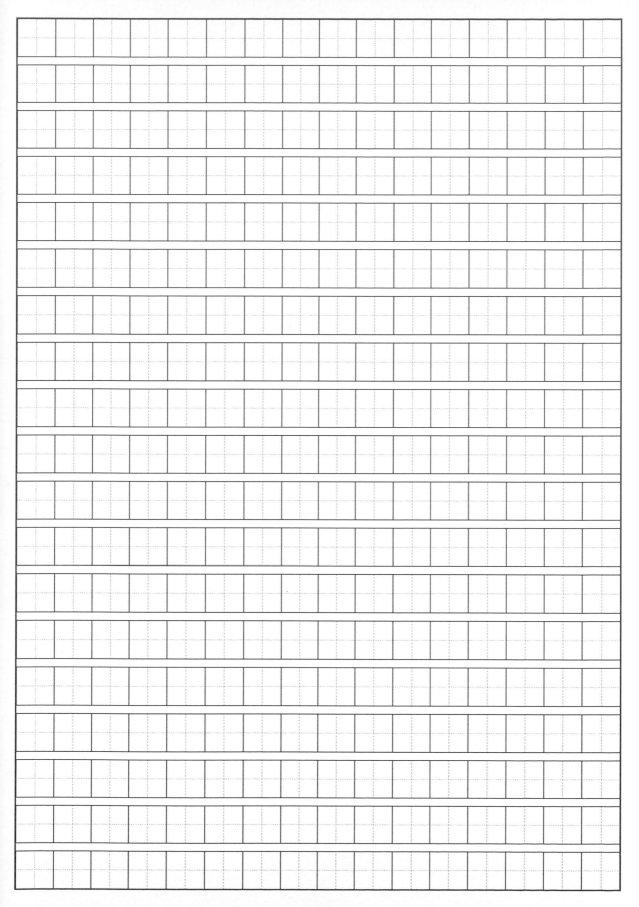

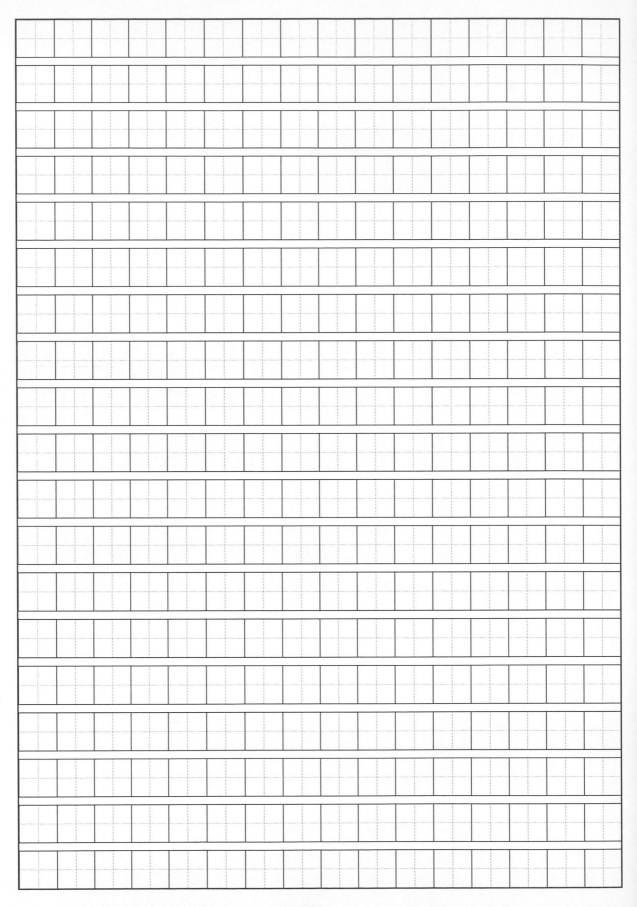

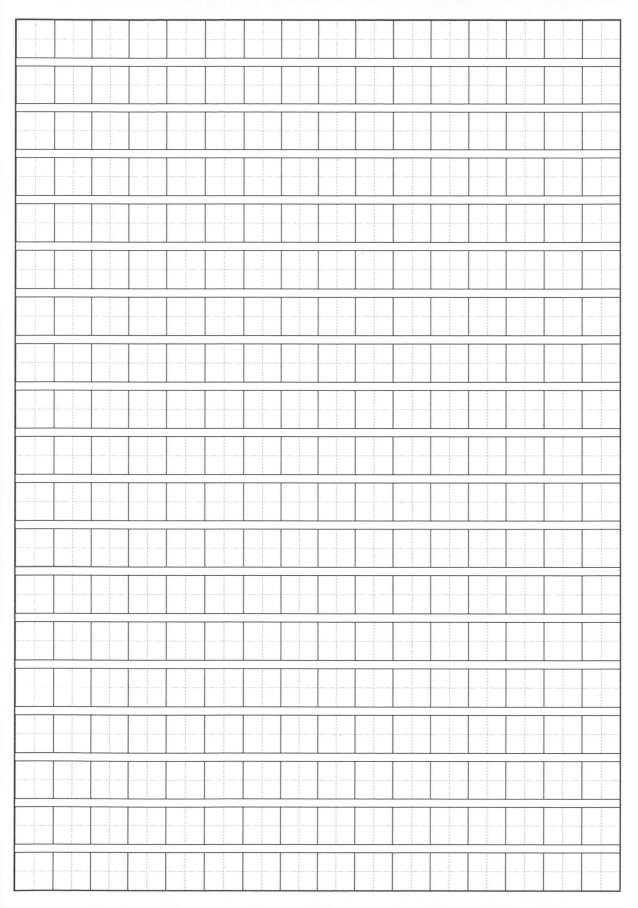

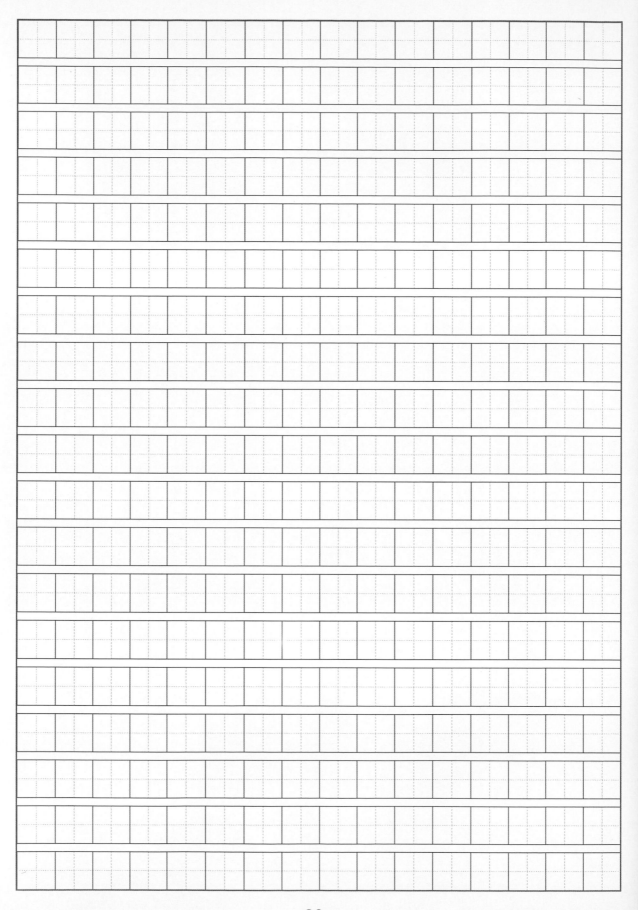

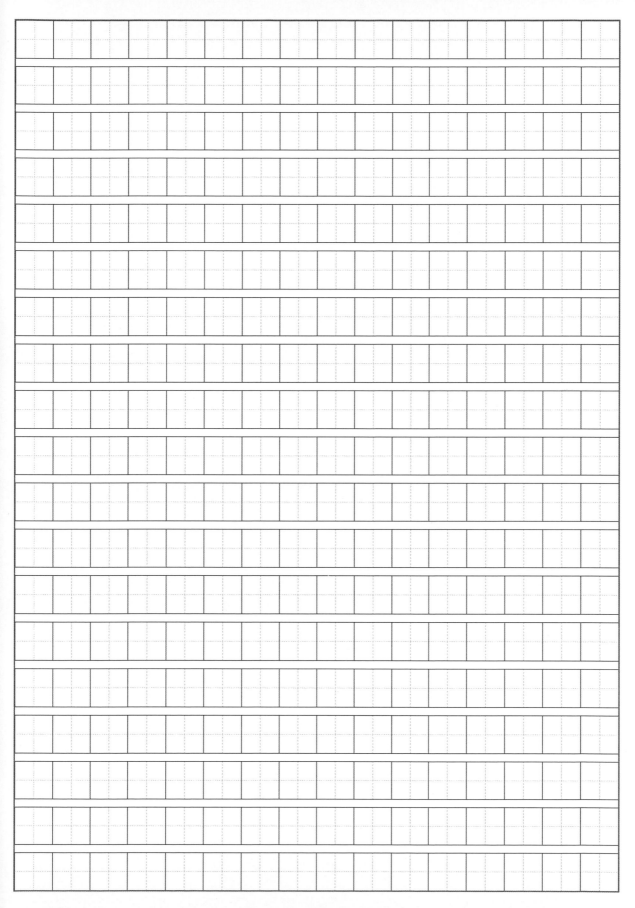

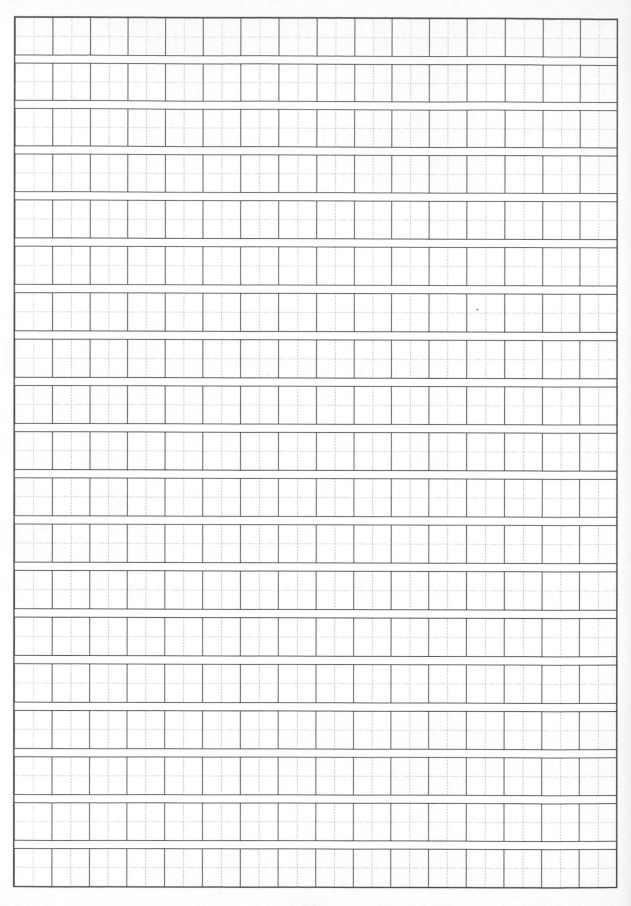

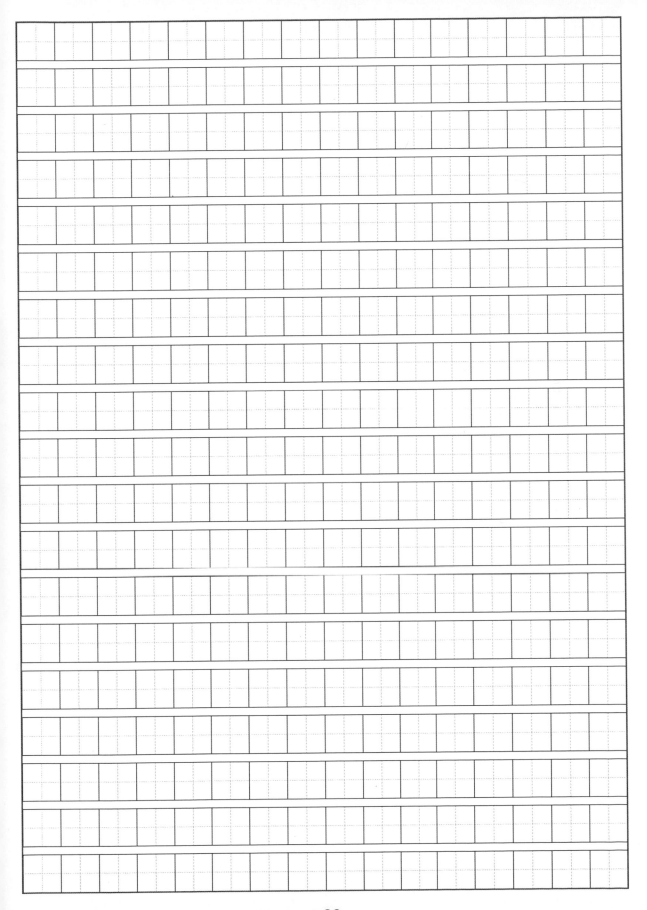

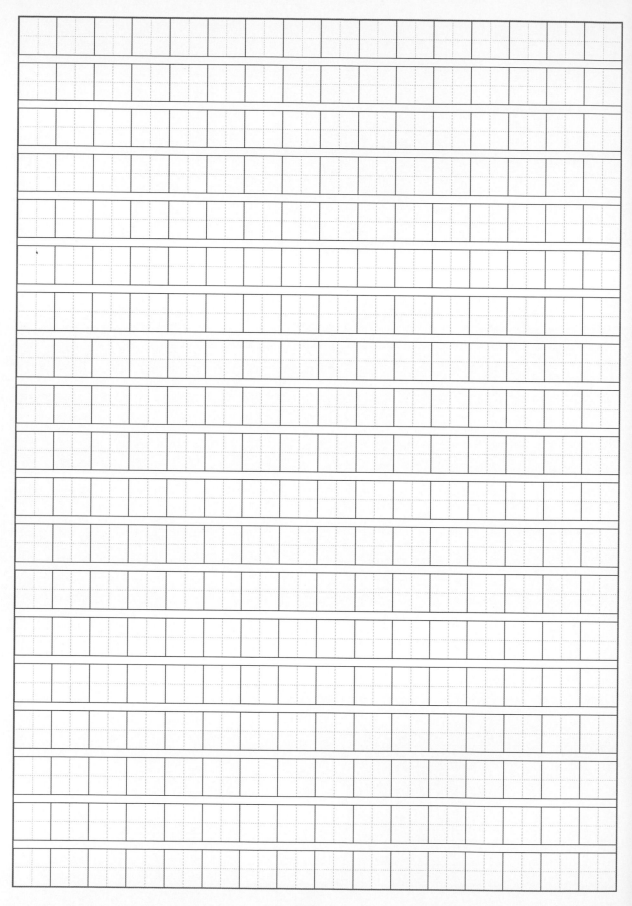

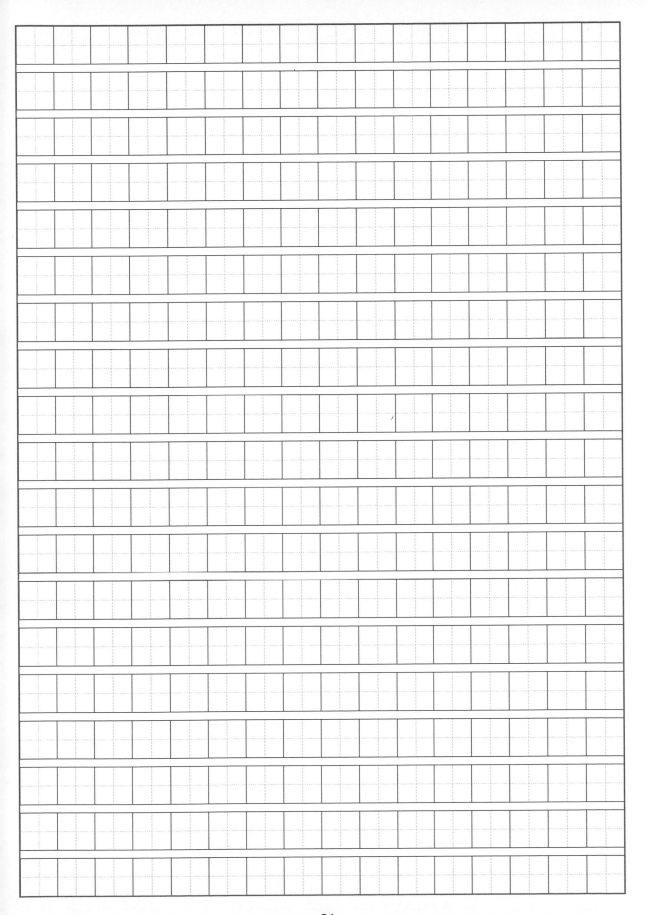

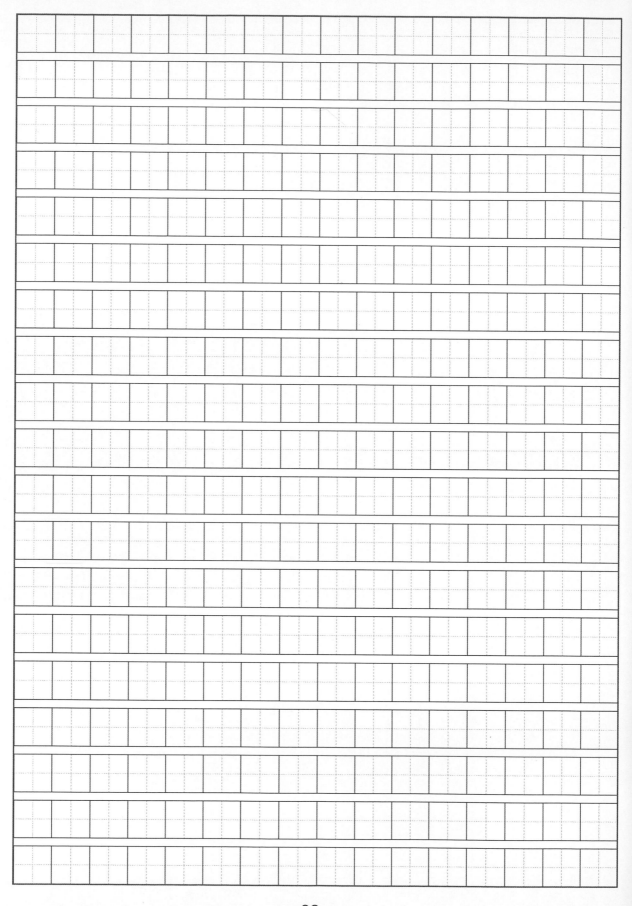

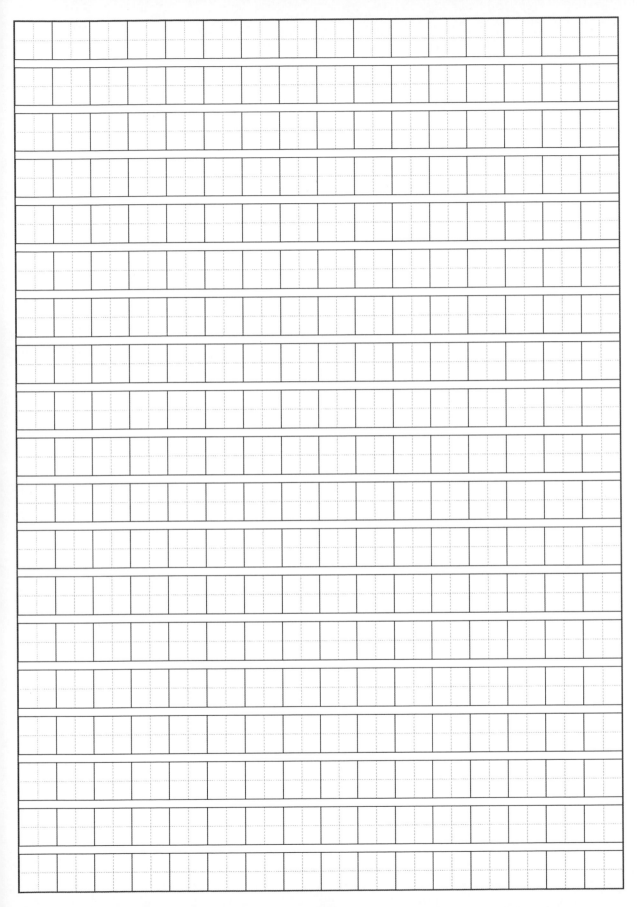

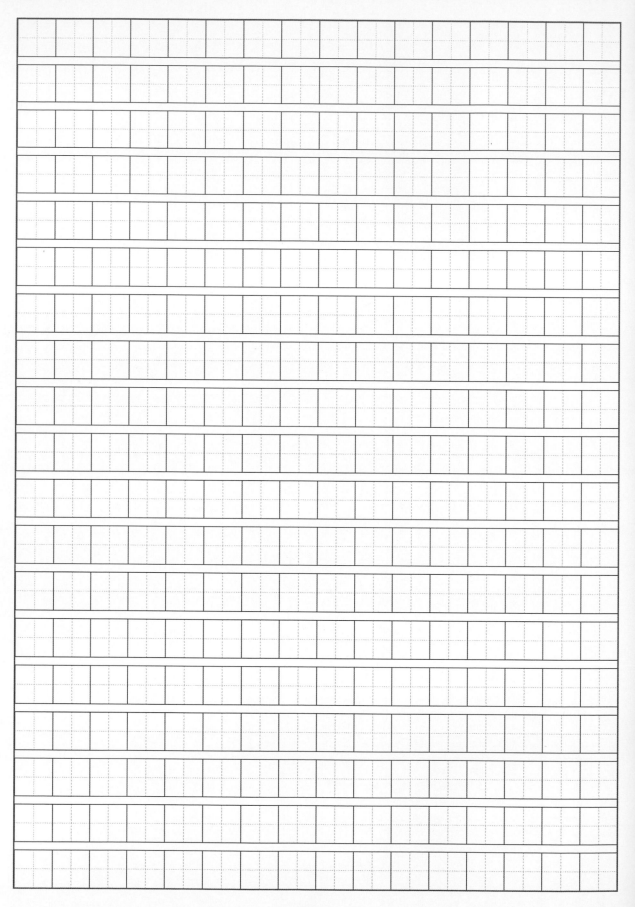

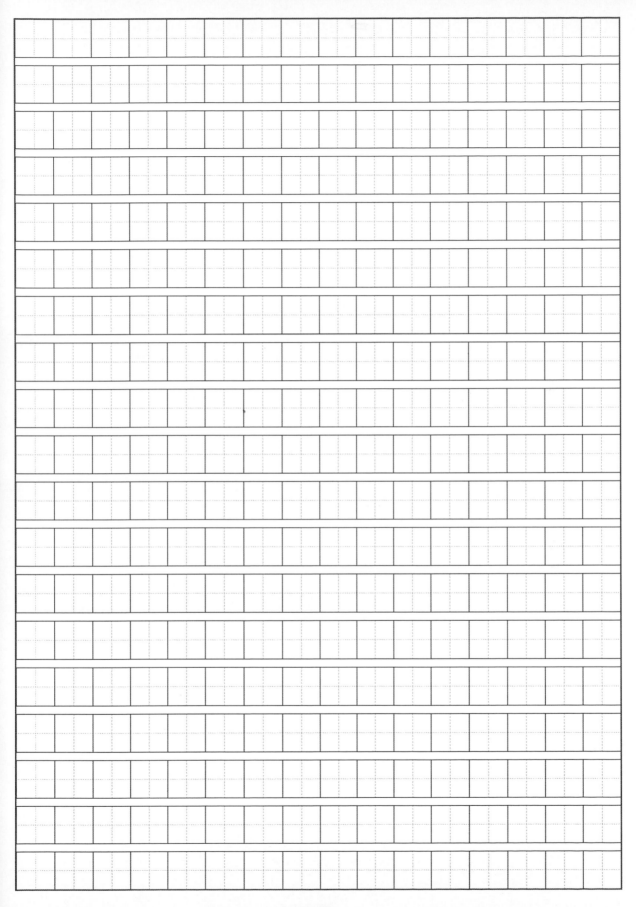

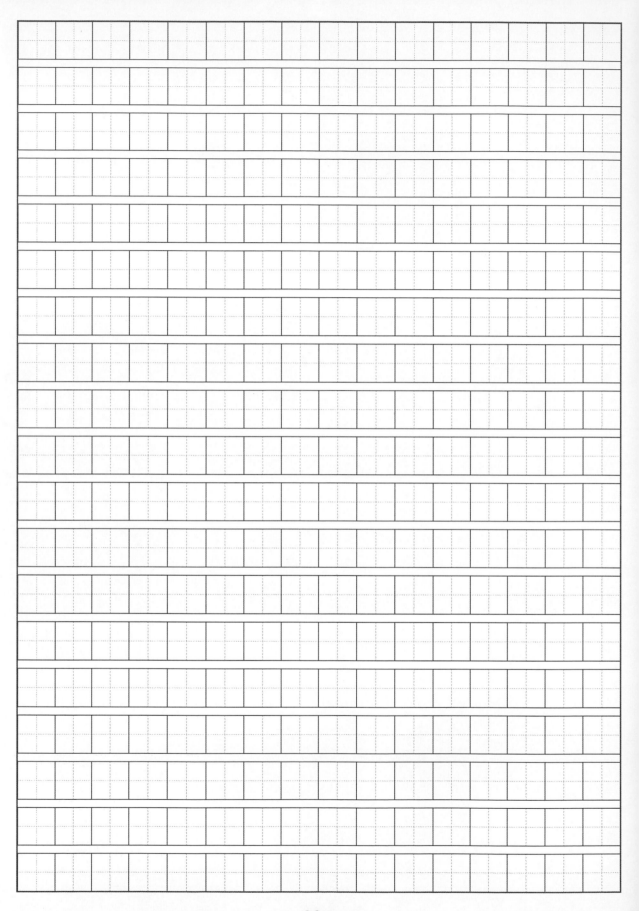

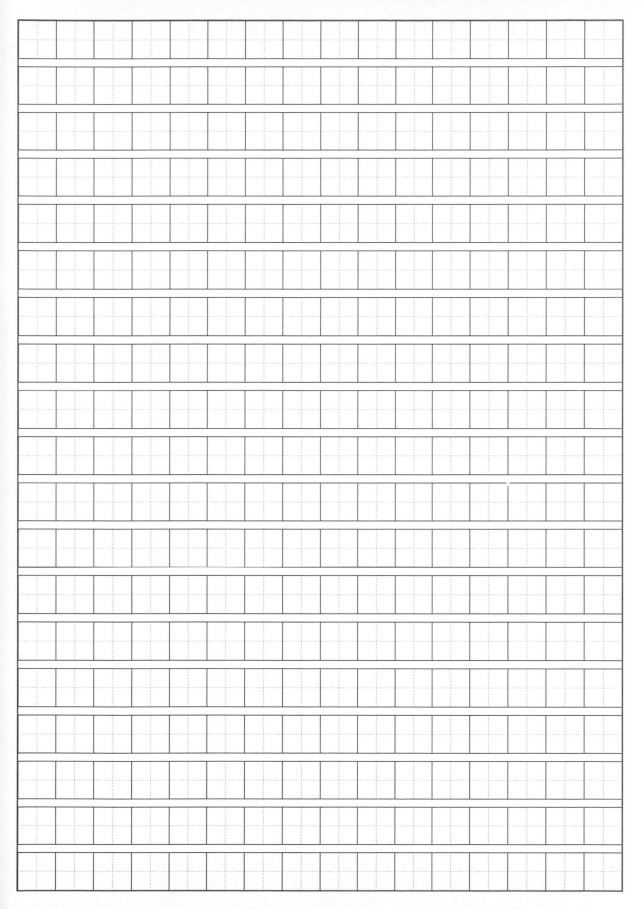

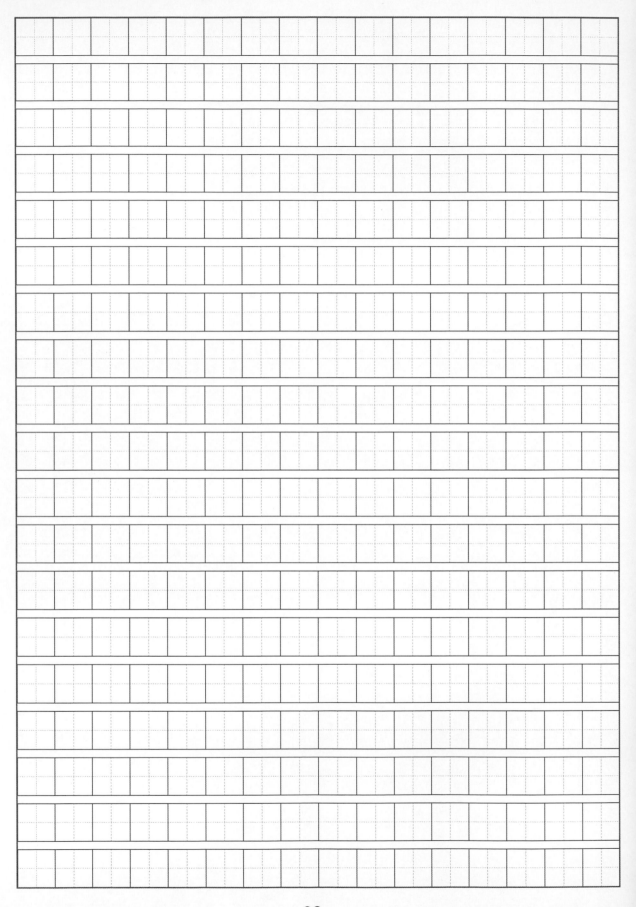

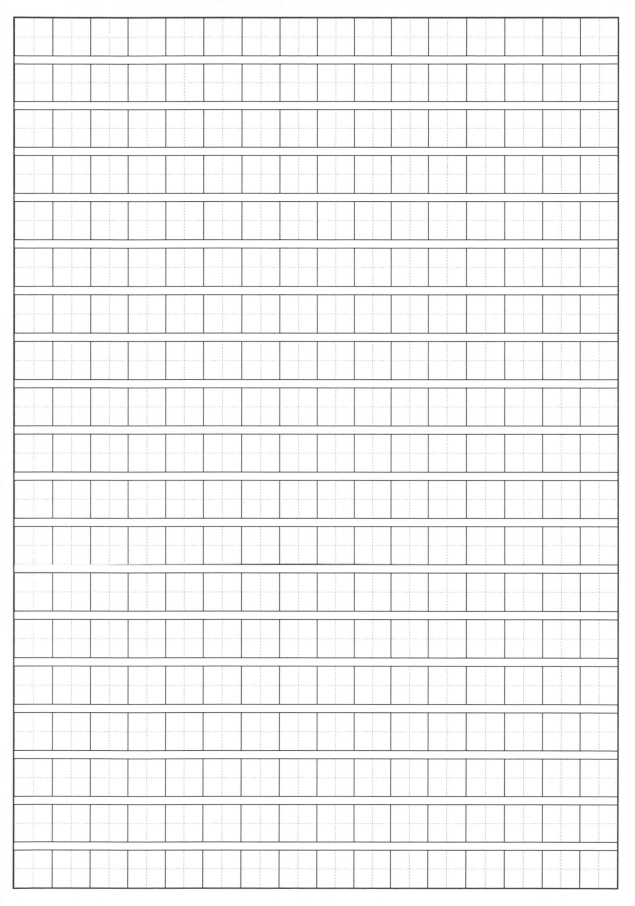

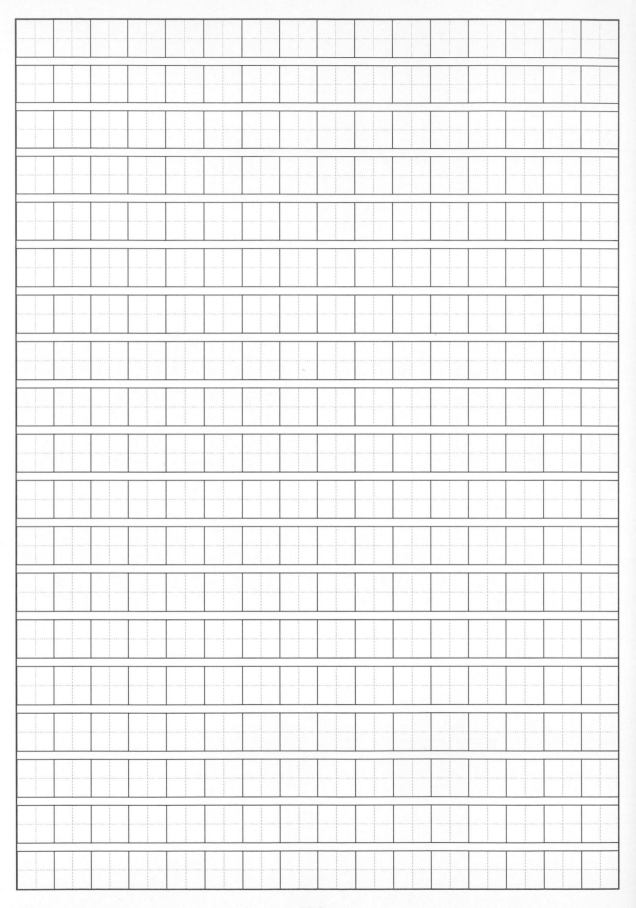

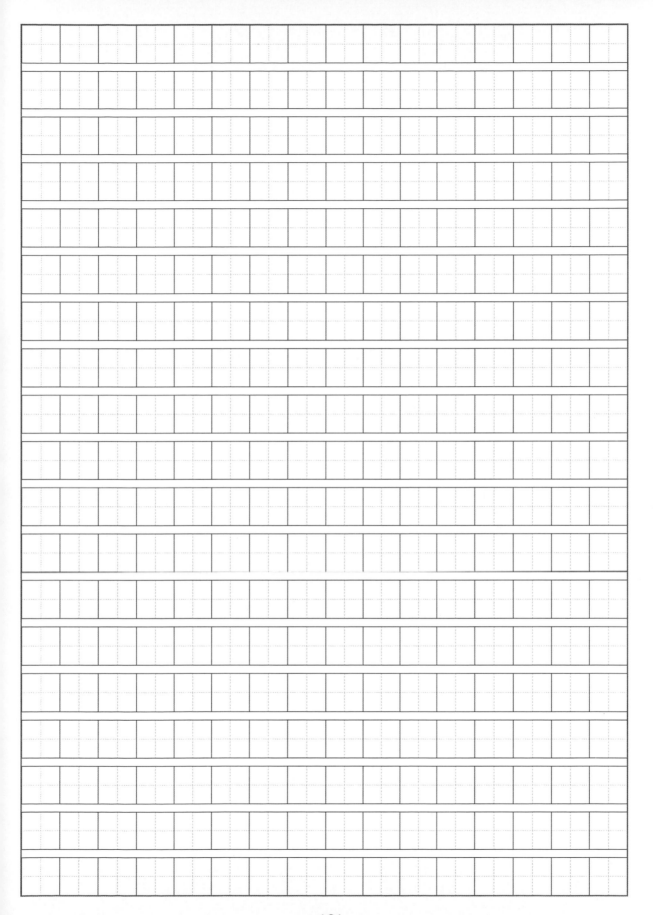

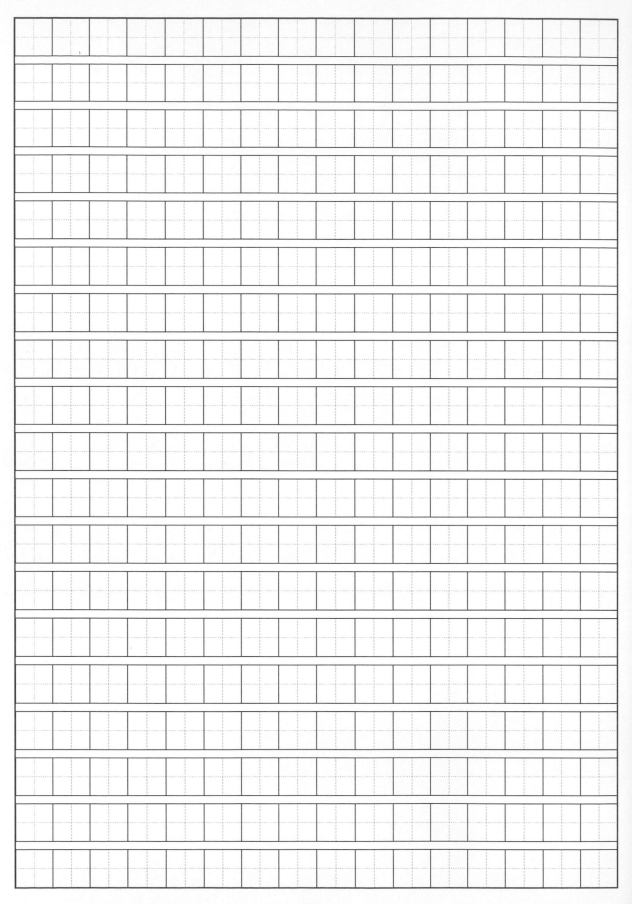

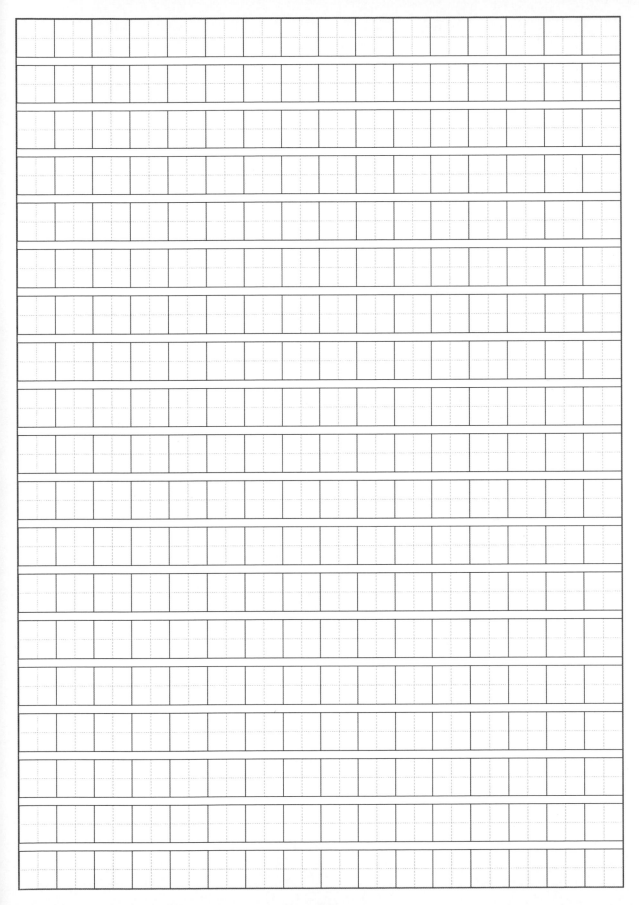

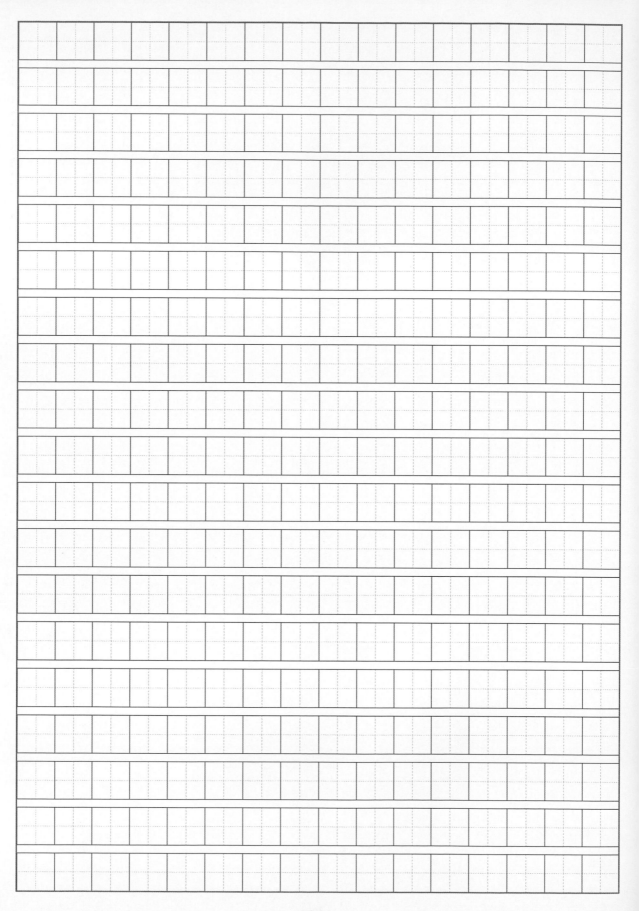

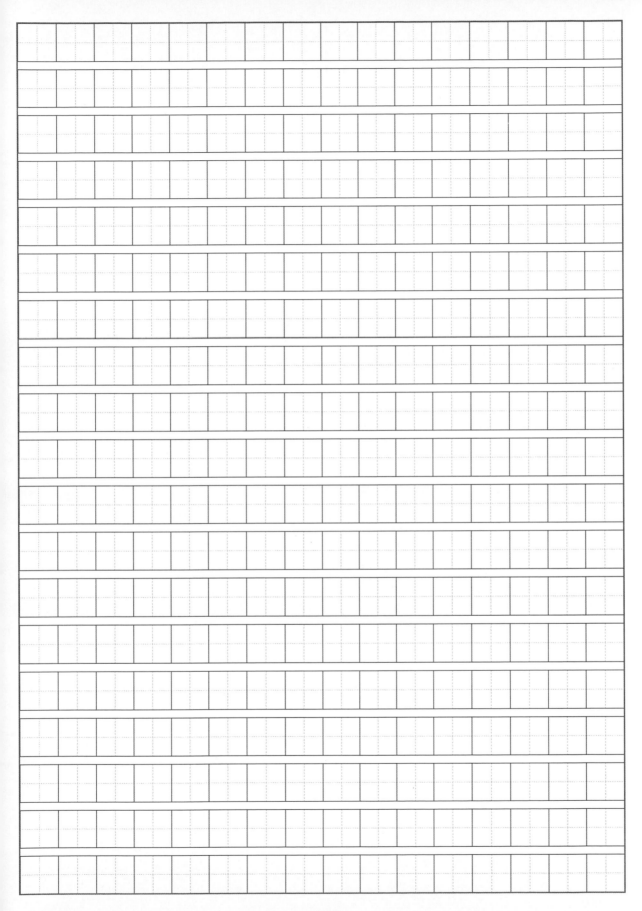

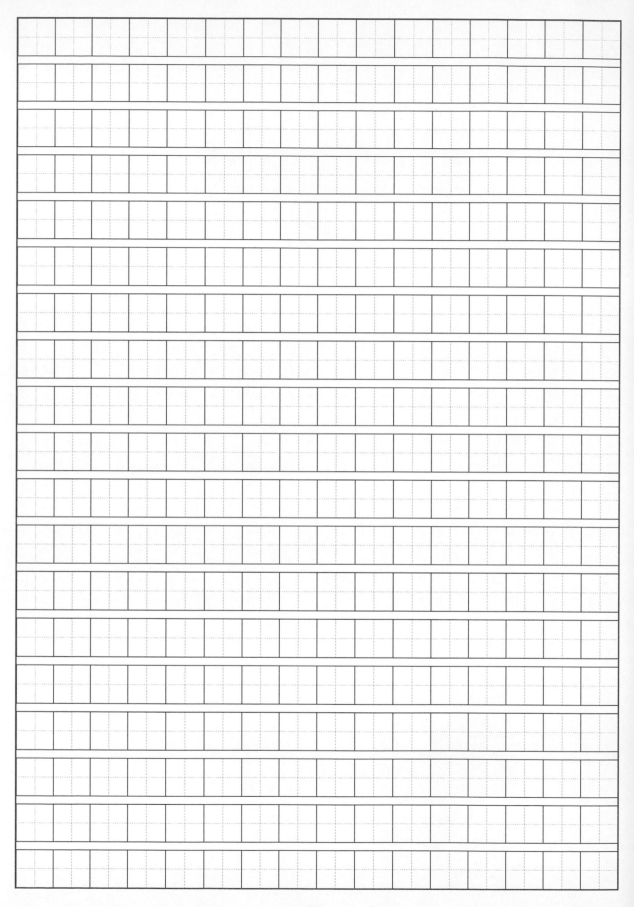

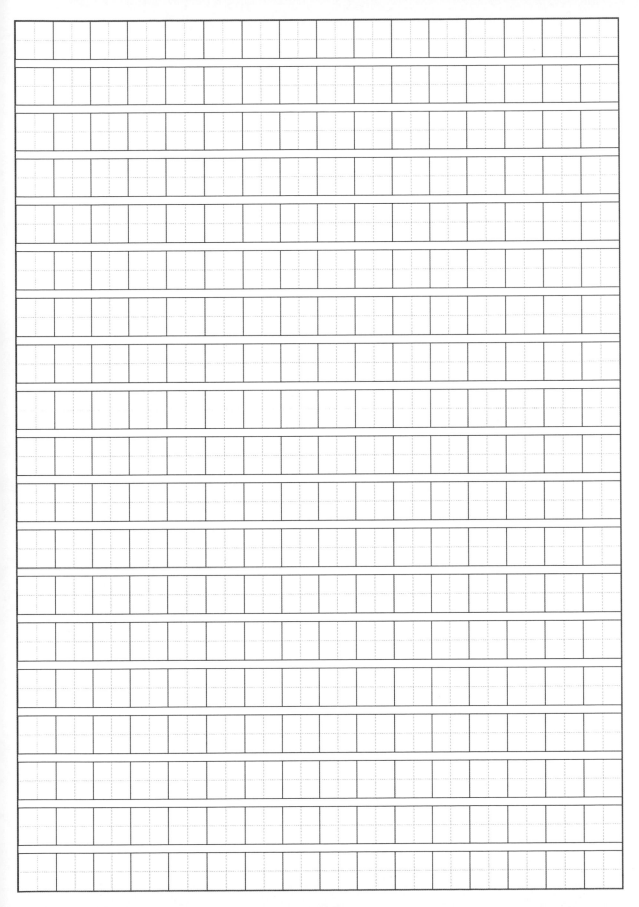

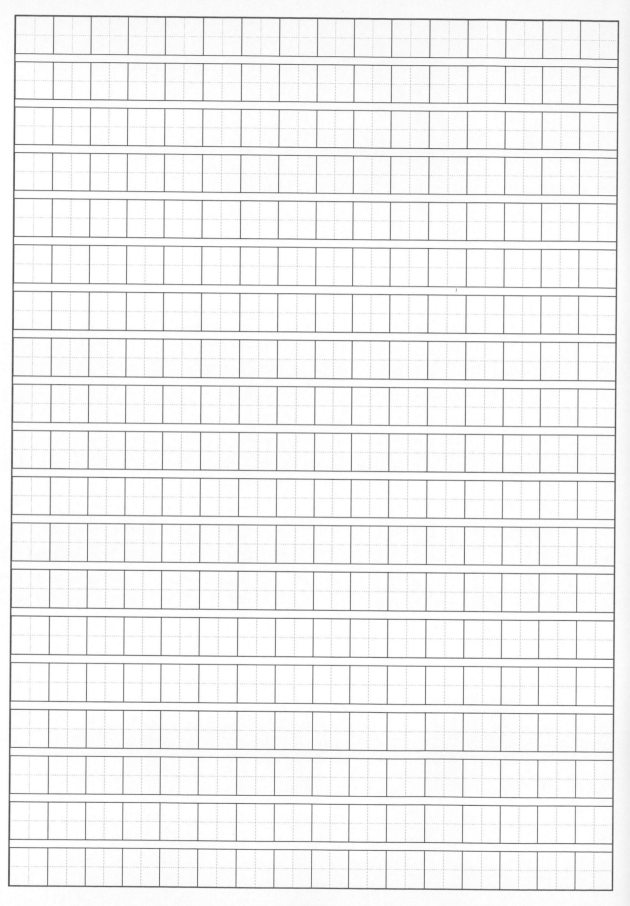

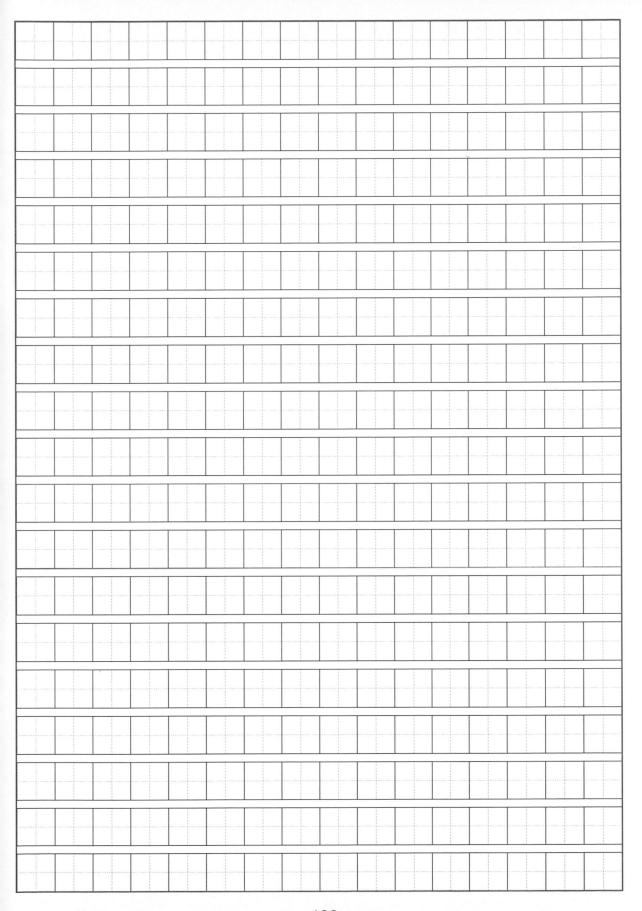

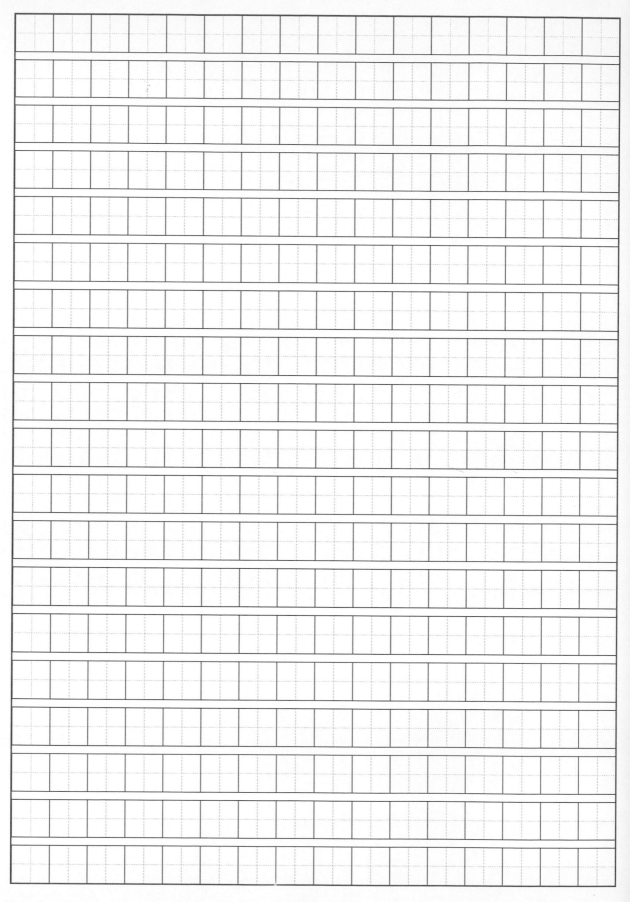

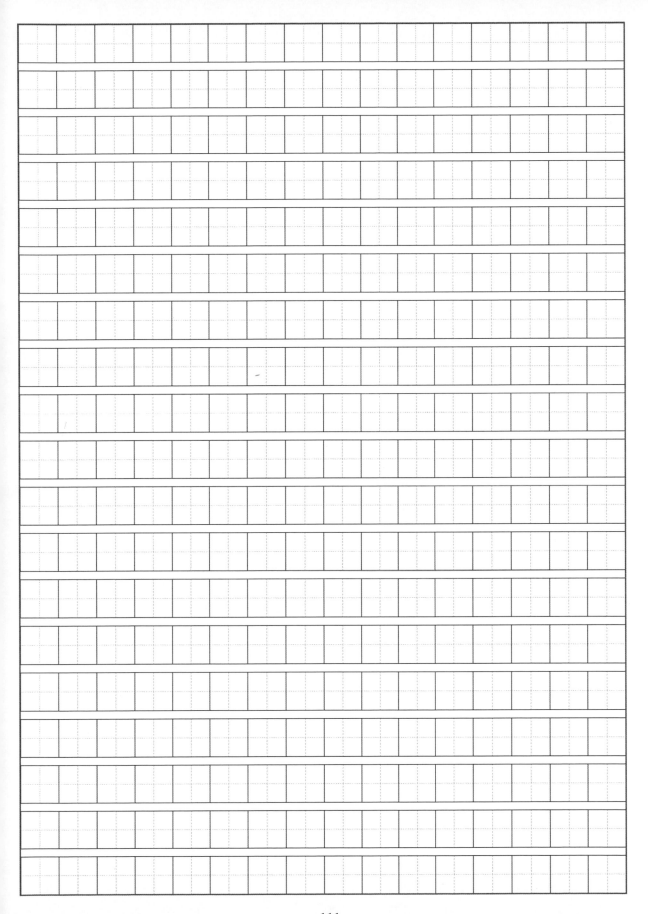

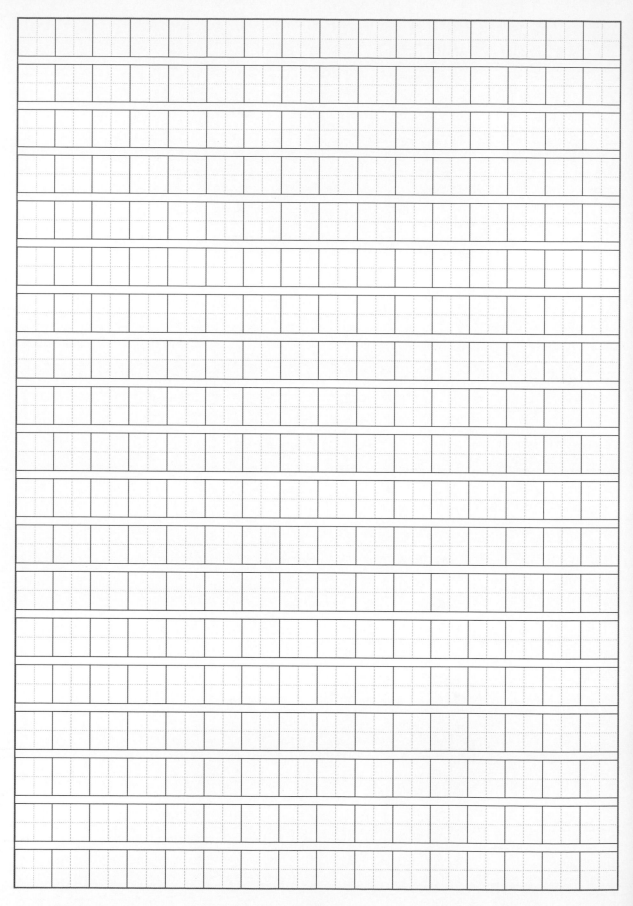

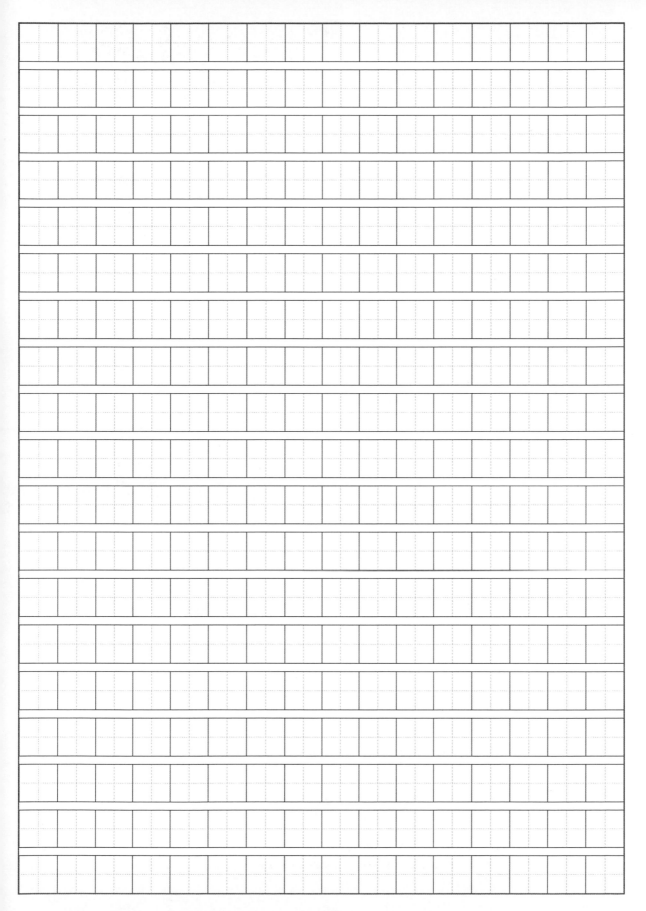

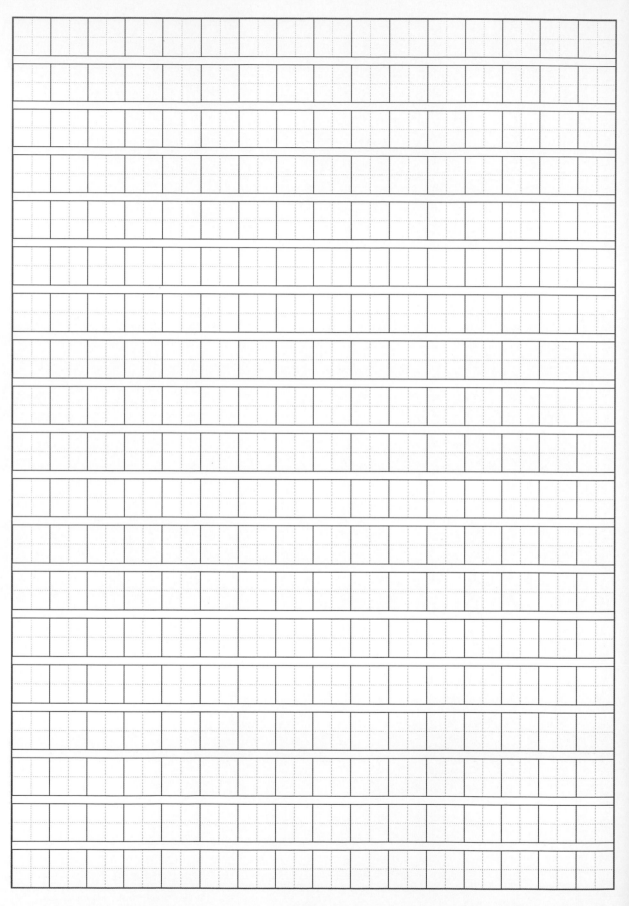

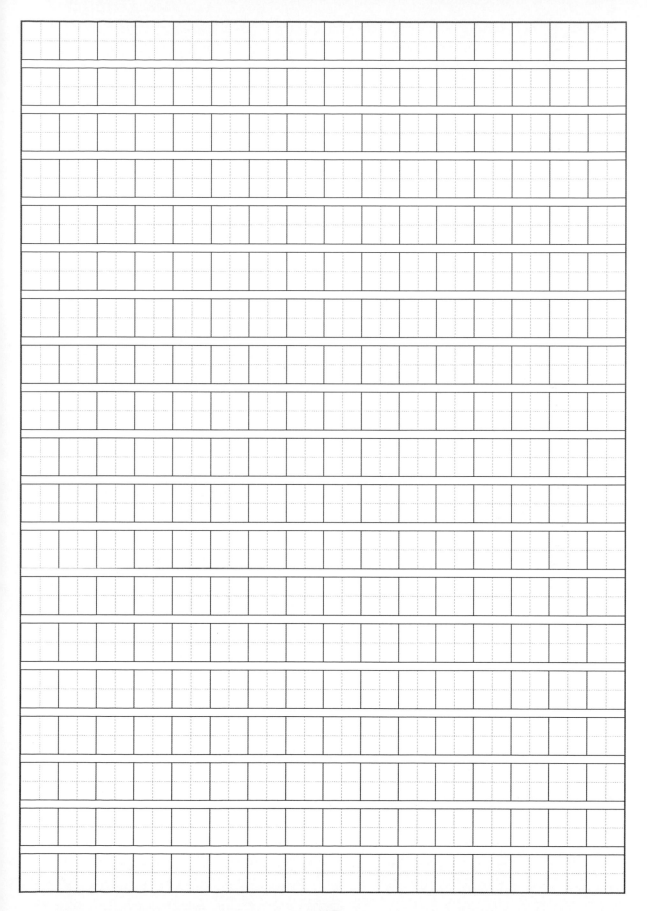

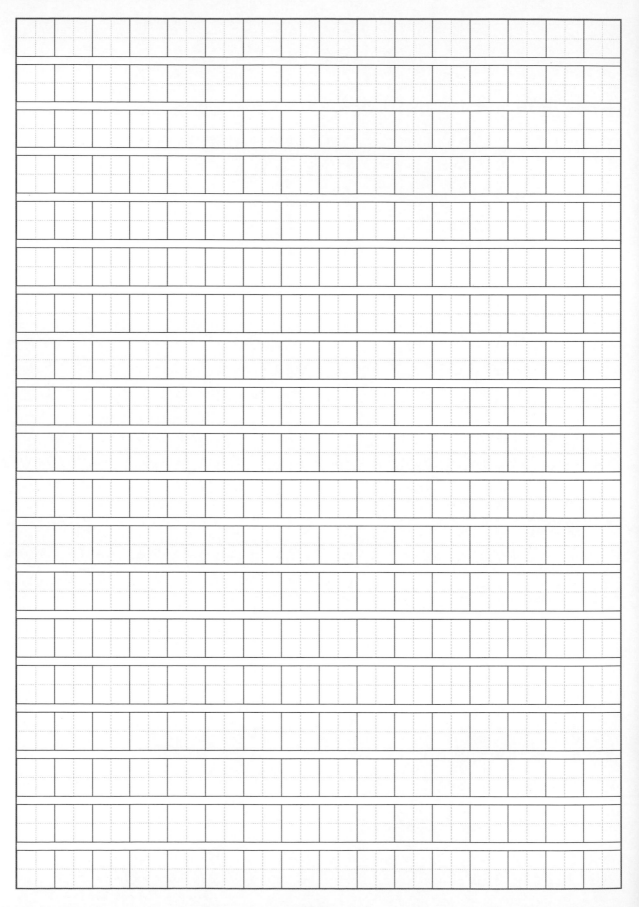

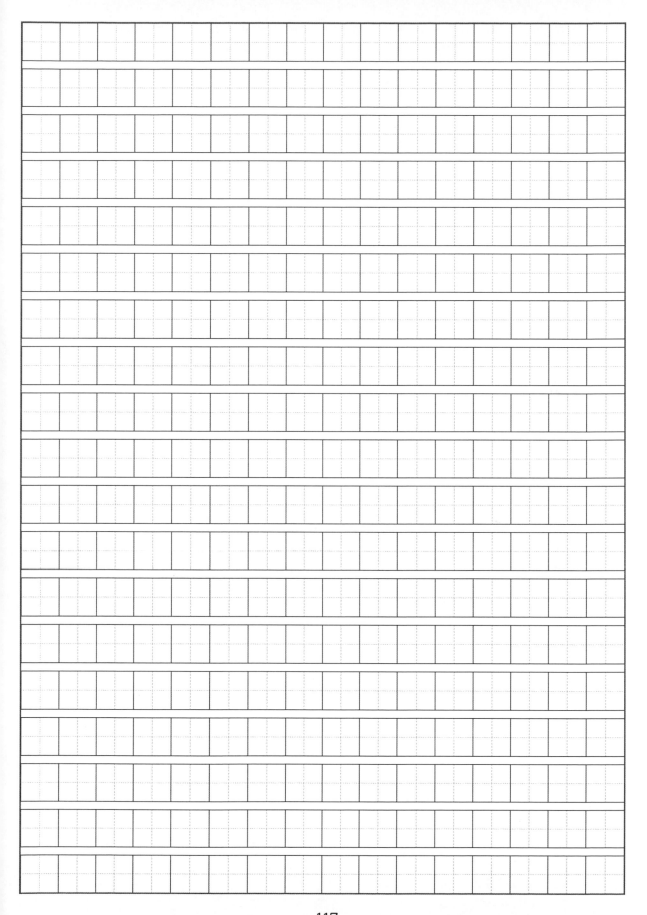

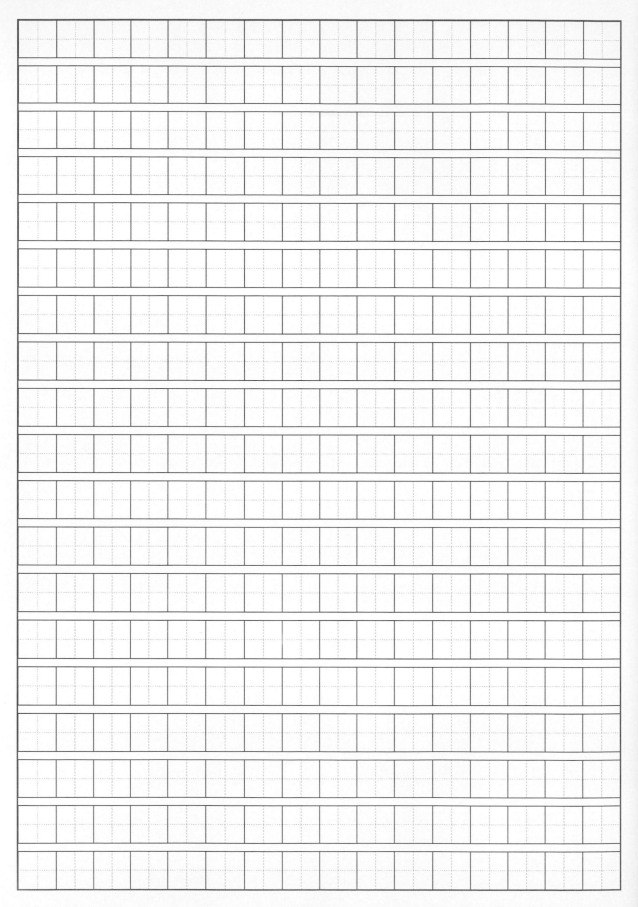

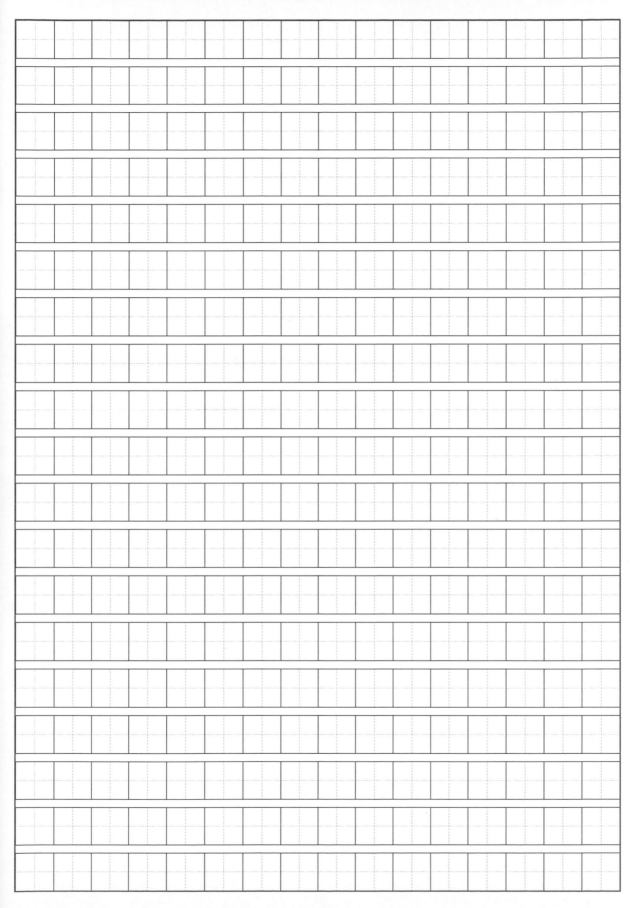

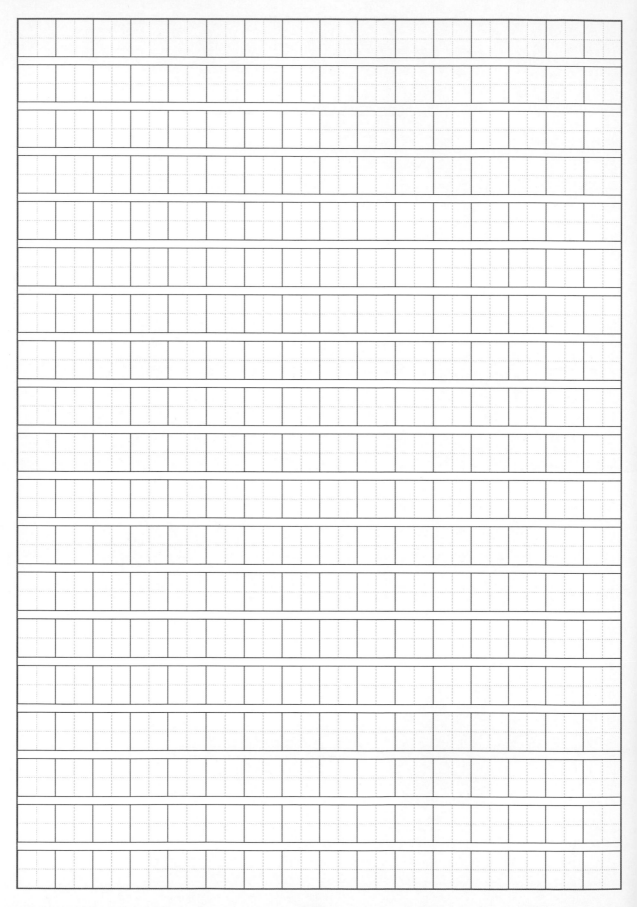

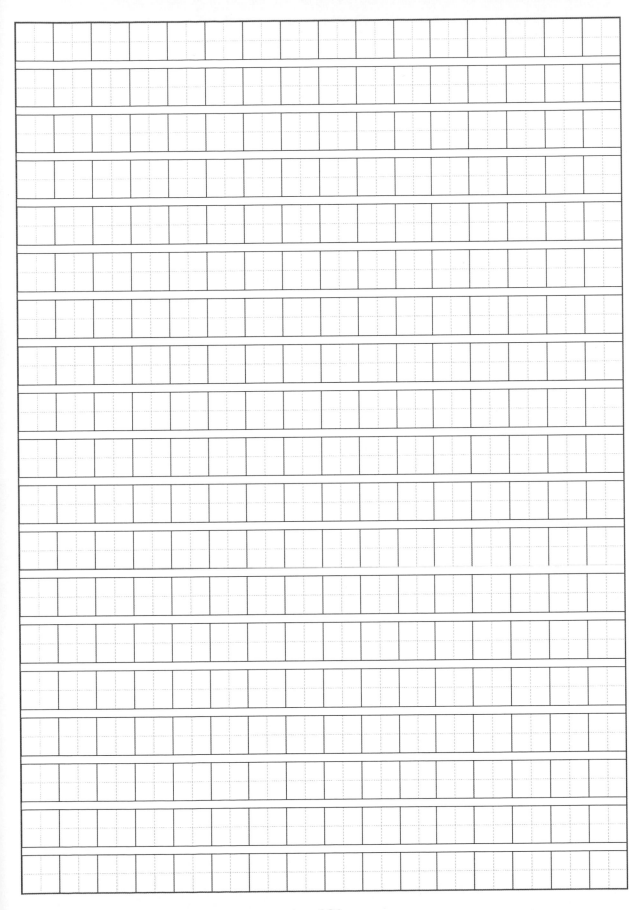

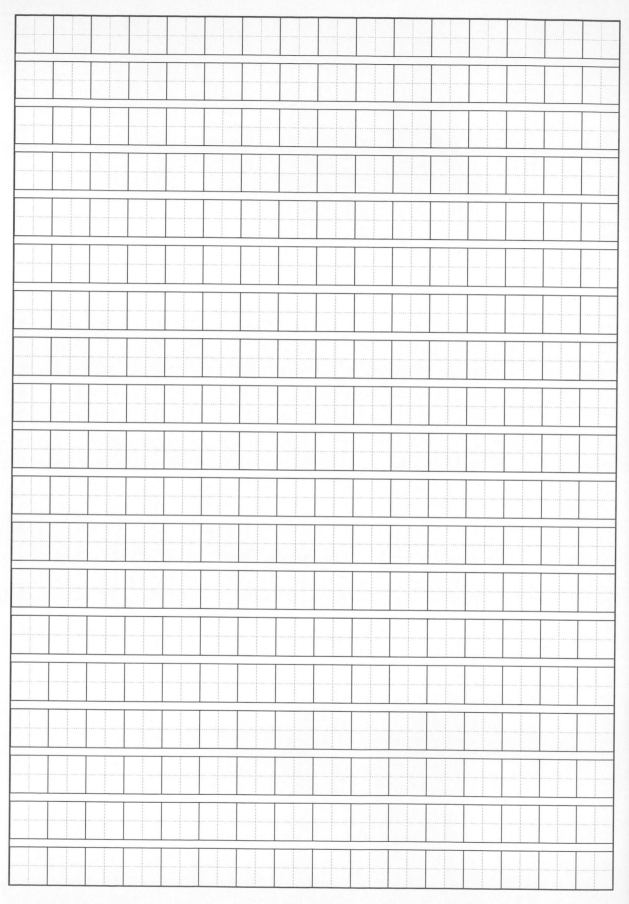

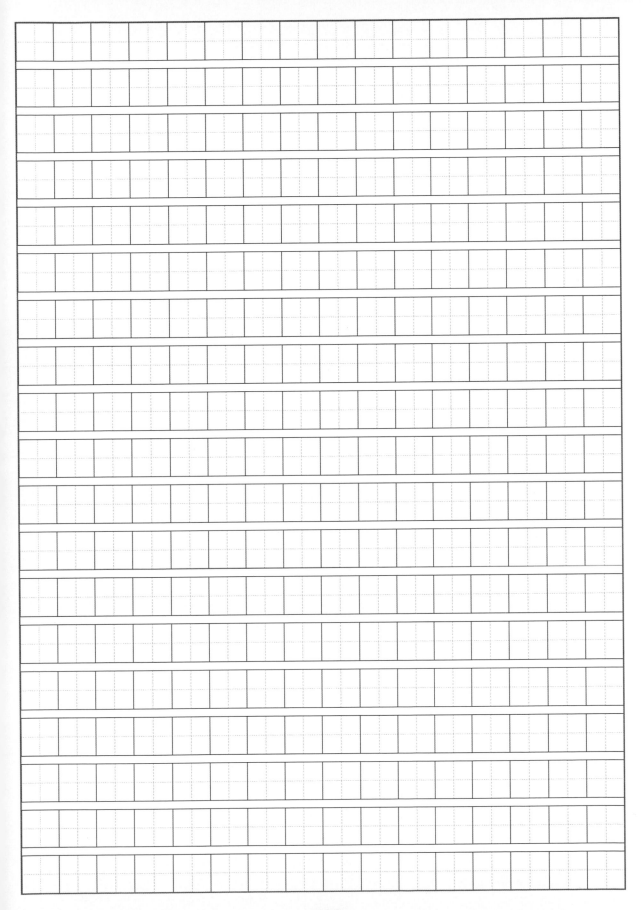

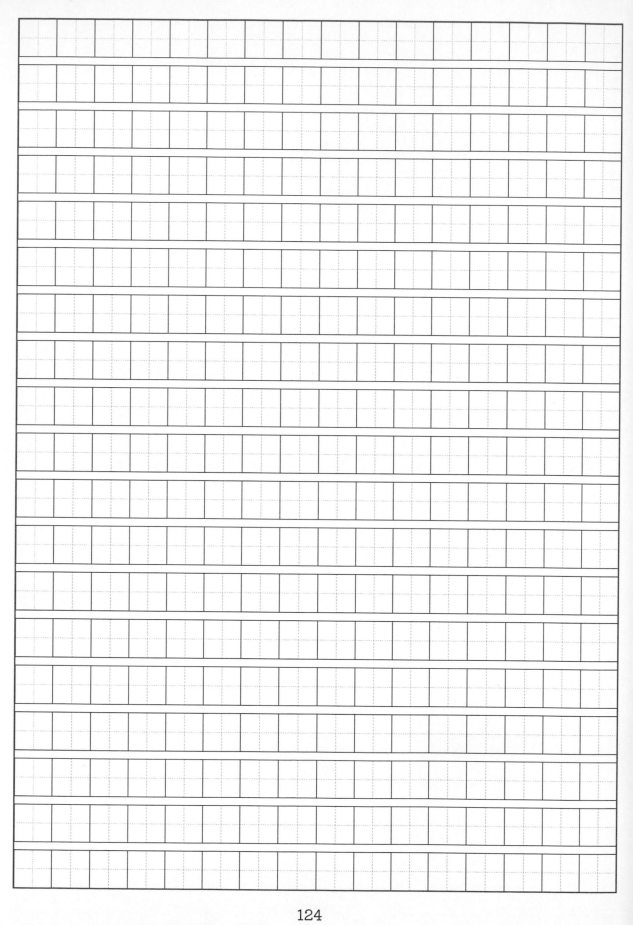

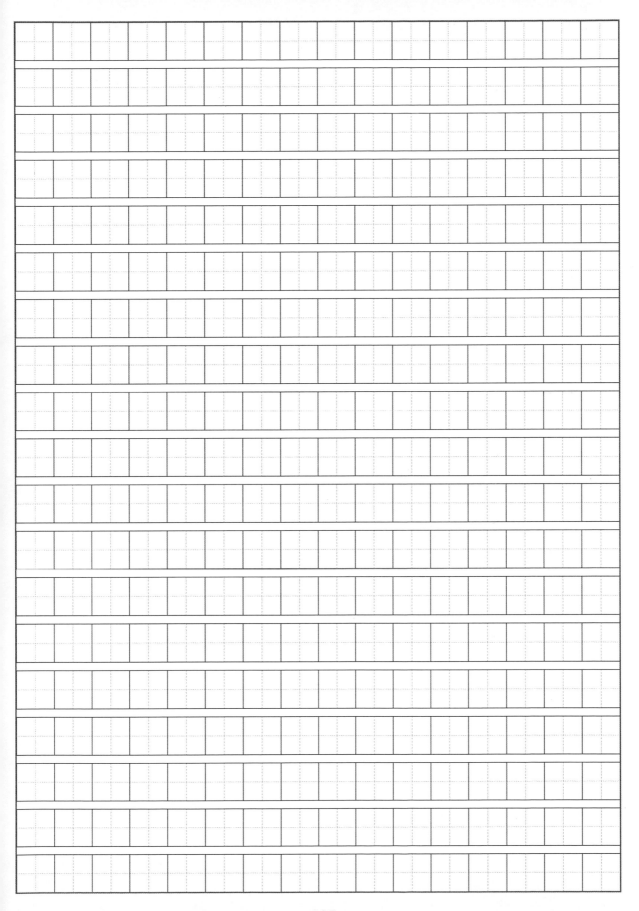

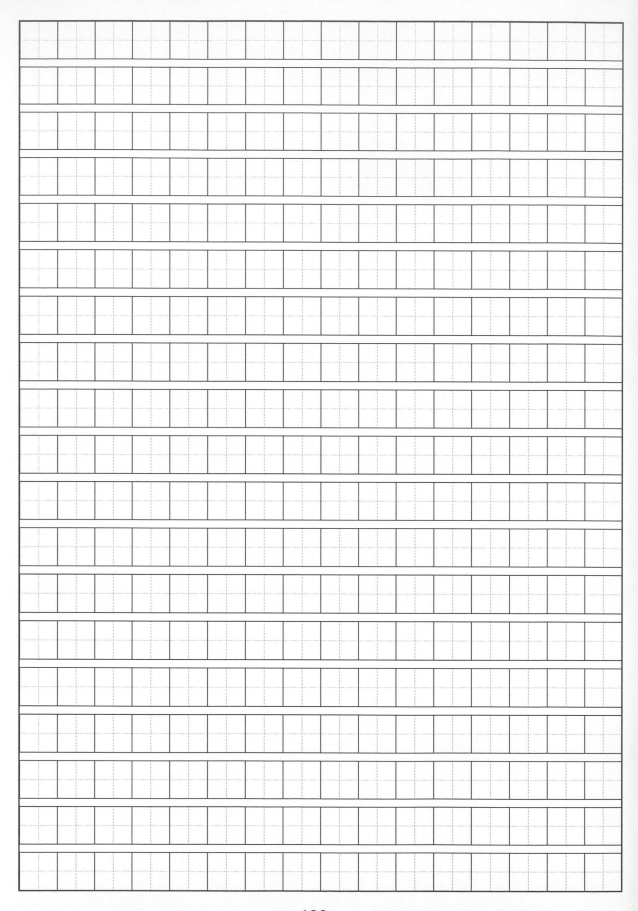

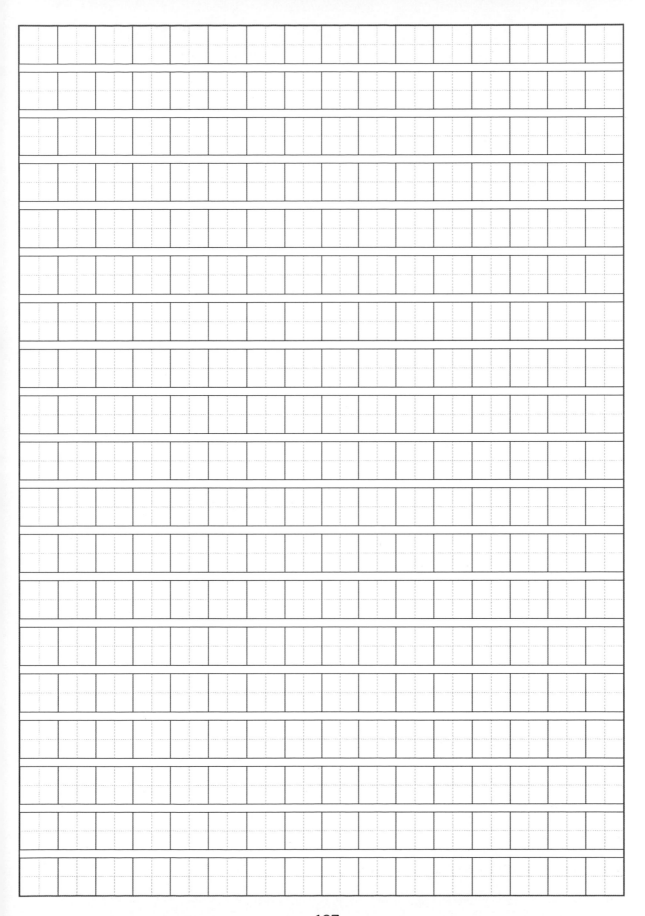

"Books to Span the East and West"

Tuttle Publishing was founded in 1832 in the small New England town of Rutland, Vermont [USA]. Our core values remain as strong today as they were then—to publish best-in-class books which bring people together one page at a time. In 1948, we established a publishing outpost in Japan—and Tuttle is now a leader in publishing English-language books about the arts, languages and cultures of Asia. The world has become a much smaller place today and Asia's economic and cultural influence has grown. Yet the need for meaningful dialogue and information about this diverse region has never been greater. Over the past seven decades, Tuttle has published thousands of books on subjects ranging from martial arts and paper crafts to language learning and literature—and our talented authors, illustrators, designers and photographers have won many prestigious awards. We welcome you to explore the wealth of information available on Asia at www.tuttlepublishing.com. at **www.tuttlepublishing.com**.

Published by Tuttle Publishing, an imprint of Periplus Editions (HK) Ltd.

www.tuttlepublishing.com

Copyright © 2023 by Periplus Editions (HK) Ltd.

ISBN 978-0-8048-5628-7

27 26 25 24 23
10 9 8 7 6 5 4 3 2 1

Printed in Singapore   2305MP

Distributed by

North America, Latin America & Europe
Tuttle Publishing
364 Innovation Drive
North Clarendon, VT 05759-9436 U.S.A.
Tel: 1 (802) 773-8930; Fax: 1 (802) 773-6993
info@tuttlepublishing.com; www.tuttlepublishing.com

Asia Pacific
Berkeley Books Pte. Ltd.
3 Kallang Sector #04-01
Singapore 349278
Tel: (65) 6741 2178; Fax: (65) 6741 2179
inquiries@periplus.com.sg; www.tuttlepublishing.com

TUTTLE PUBLISHING® is a registered trademark of Tuttle Publishing, a division of Periplus Editions (HK) Ltd.